THE
Feminine
Principle

THE KEY TO
AWAKENING FOR
MEN & WOMEN

Nurit Oren

With excerpts from Gabor Harsanyi's lectures,
interviews and Satsangs

Published by Gabor Harsanyi
Budapest, Hungary

Book cover and internal design by Jane Green of Everlasting Magic Design.
www.everlastingmagicdesign.com

Editing by Stefan Verstappen, owner of Woodbridge Press

Book cover and bio pictures of Nurit Oren and Gabor Harsanyi by Eva Harsanyi

ISBN – 978-615-00-2114-0

Acknowledgements

I wish to express my undying gratitude for the many gifts of assistance I received, directly or indirectly, from the wonderful friends, who have generously and selflessly contributed to the creation of this book.

These gifts include:

- Technical support from **Gabor Gaspar**... thank you, dude... couldn't have done it without your help.

- Beautiful back cover write-up and proof reading this book by **Stefan Verstappen**, author of A Masters Guide to The Way of the Warrior.

- Inner and outer book design by **Jane Green** of Everlasting Magic Design... love your work. It is truly magical, and since I keep coming back to you, it must be everlasting.

- The front cover picture and bio pictures by our beloved cousin, **Eva Harsanyi**... what a gifted photographer! You can even make me look good!

- Interviews that provided great excerpts for this book by: **Iain McNay** of Conscious.TV; author and coach **Stefan Hiene**; and spiritual coach and couple & family therapist, **Anna Lena Eldoey Nygaard**.

- Satsang support and great conversation-inducing questions by our dear London partners, **Yannick** and **Ben Mango**.

- Permission to use an insightful story by my daughter, **Shirit Oren**.

- Love and support from our dear friend **Pierre Richard**, who provided countless recorded conversations with Gabor, and who introduced to us spiritual mentor, **Susanne Marie**.

- The moving *Foreword* by our dear friend **Susanne Marie**... a humble giant among female teachers.

- The wonderful inspiration that sprang from a conversation with the lovely **Susanne Marie** and **Gabor Harsanyi** - a conversation, without which, this book could never see the light of day.

- The loving and patient mentorship and countless hours of inspiring conversations by my beloved life partner, best friend and teacher, **Gabor Harsanyi**.

Table of Contents

CHAPTER FOUR
SETTING FREE OUR GIFT OF ATTENTION

CHAPTER FIVE
PURSUEING OUR QUEENDOM IS NOT FOR WIMPS

CHAPTER SIX
LIVING LIFE FROM OUR QUEENDOM

CHAPTER SEVEN
LAW OF ATTRACTION IS NOT WHAT WE 'THINK'

CHAPTER EIGHT
BACK TO UTOPIA

Resources

QR Code Reading

The books and all the videos mentioned in this book can be accessed by reading the QR Codes below. To do so, you will need to have a QR Code reader on your mobile phone. You can download a QR Code reader from the App Store or Google Play by typing "QR Code reader" into the search.

 **Video Access**

To access the videos mentioned in this book use this QR Code.

 **Books Access**

To access Nurit's book *"The Blind Leading the Blonde on the Road to Freedom: Confessions of a Recovering Spiritual Junkie"* use this QR Code.

 To access Gabor's book *"Functional Silence: De-mystifying Awakening for the Spiritually Exhausted"* use this QR Code.

 **YouTube Access**

To access the YouTube channel of Gabor and Nurit, use this QR Code.

THE Feminine Principle

THE KEY TO AWAKENING FOR MEN & WOMEN

Nurit Oren

With excerpts from Gabor Harsanyi's lectures,
interviews and Satsangs

Foreword

I have found so many gems within the pages of Nurit Oren's book, *The Feminine Principle: The Key to Awakening for Men and Women*. As the title suggests, this refreshing book is about accessing the feminine principle, which we all contain within, and how it is imperative if we wish to live our potentiality and awaken on a personal as well as global level. Our planet and humanity are what are at stake here, says Nurit, and what is being asked by life itself is that we earnestly begin paying attention to the ways in which we are out of touch with our own bodies and inner Being. Both Nurit and her husband, Gabor, are dedicated to assisting the sincere reader in the return Home. This is where we all meet in Truth, where individuality opens up to a larger connected whole where pure possibility lives.

Through her writing, Nurit has a way of bringing the reader into the depth of what she herself has realized. Everything is fair game and no topic is too taboo for her to pick apart or dive into. She is sincere almost to a fault, and her humor and honest self-assessment makes for a romping good read. While carrying the reader along a river in a sort of merry way, the book offers wisdom of the sort that comes out of real life experience, demonstrating that understanding is available to us at whatever level one is willing to take it in. This is the gift of Nurit's writing. From what I can tell, it is an intrinsic part of who she is: open, honest, wise, full of heart and at times just plain frankly funny.

I would like to say something about humor. True humor born out of the caldron of difficult life experience and alchemized into something fluid, light, and effervescent, is an actual art form. Nurit has it in spades. Within these pages you will find a delightful balance of all the ingredients that make for a good read, including the lighter side. At the same time, the reader is halted, spellbound, wishing to savor a certain passage that conveys and contains rich texture, nuance, and depth to it.

Nurit is definitely *not* a lightweight when it comes to waking us up out of our mind-numbing slumber. When speaking about what is being asked of us at this time, she writes: "A new course is required now. By redirecting our attention away from the thought-stream and into the body through feeling... with no expectation... we activate the transformative nature of the body. We shift from relaxing in the mind to resting in the heart through the feminine-like feeling of pure being. This is your queendom." In other words, "We need to get out of our heads and into our bodies," and I couldn't agree more!

So, why are the qualities that we associate with our feminine nature so important at this time? We live in a world that places its core values on what we can get from others and out of life. In this way we turn ourselves, others, and the Earth into a commodity (as something separate from ourselves). As a result, we are starved for soul, for intimacy and true connection with one another, as well as for feeling our interconnectedness to the Earth that we are a part of. In order to shift the habitual trance-like outgoing attention of consciousness we need tools to help us remember our way back home, as within lies the primary connection. Nurit writes: "The direction is *in* and the space is the silence of *being*."

What I especially like about Nurit's book, is that it contains an interesting mixture of her story (who doesn't like a good story?), along with wise and radical ideas that are frankly feminist in nature (without leaving men out of the equation, which is another art form), as well as how to reach toward what she and Gabor are both pointing to: redirecting attention to one's Being-Nature held within the body.

Within our bodies is infinite wisdom and intelligence. The body does not lie. Within our natural form is the mystery of existence itself, and this mystery is accessible when we learn to place our attention on what is arising without moving or pushing it away. Then, what is always available, the silence of Being that is contained within matter, within the body, has a chance to reveal itself; and when we open to what is revealed, the true transformative power of life-force alchemizes and revitalizes whatever is in the way of our inner freedom. This type of leaning-into our inner being is feminine in nature as it requires stillness, a quality of openness, and a willingness to stop the outward movement of mind in surrender to the inner stillness of body. Nurit explains: 'The feminine type of awakening is about release, surrender, letting go, submission to the 'moment-to-moment'ness of presence, acceptance of silence over our well-developed intellectual templates, the willingness to convert the way we think and feel and much more'.

Nurit states that it's time to reclaim our 'queendom', one in which no one (man or woman), is left out. That the shift into embracing our feminine nature is biologically imperative if the human race is meant to continue. Anything short of realizing that the Earth's body is our own, and that all of life is precious, valuable, and worthy of protecting, will bring about our downfall and many innocent life-forms with us.

There is no way around the fact that this book is a call to go within to access the inner body, and it becomes quite clear why this is so important. If you haven't yet discovered for yourself the peace within, I suspect that this book will inspire you to check it out for yourself. And if you are in need of deeper support, the teachings and sharing in these pages can fill that need by helping you find your own way home. Nurit and Gabor's dedication to empowering individuals to find out for themselves what is true demonstrates the ultimate sign of authenticity.

Susanne Marie
Spiritual Mentor

Introduction

If someone would have asked me six months ago if I would consider writing a book on a 'feminine' topic, they would receive a resounding "NOT!" There were at least three or four major residual influences stemming from my spiritual 'salad days' that would have contributed to this response.

A. Male teachers who shamelessly belittled women.

B. Being surrounded by female bosses who compensated for their feminine insecurities by exuding and imposing false masculine energy through their positions of power. (I used to label them 'bitches,' but I now understand them.)

C. I was totally into transcending... well, pretty much anything that resembled being human as opposed to (recognize the duality here?) being a divinely spiritual person.

D. In my 'transcendental' and false non-duality phase I became a proponent of the 'androgen' as opposed to the male-female pair of opposites. In my limited spiritual mind, I believed that a transcendent human-being would most likely morph into being 'androgynous.' This belief promoted a false concept of oneness in contradistinction to the twoness of the male and female genders.

For years I had not given any thought to all this, as I was focused on my shift from spirituality to awakening. However, somehow the feelings I had about this topic seemed to remain buried within me in seed form and would, at times, rear their ugly heads at the sight of angry and hateful women who were screaming and complaining about being victimized by men whom they categorized as brutal pigs.

And then our dear friend Pierre Richard from Montreal, after having deep and meaningful conversations with Gabor, introduced us to the wonderful spiritual mentor, Susanne Marie. I watched her interview with Renate McNay on Conscious.TV and was extremely impressed. After meeting Susanne online, Gabor and I instantly became very fond of Susanne and recognized the extraordinary mutual affability between us. I especially liked the fact that she works so effectively with women.

As a result, I created a video of a conversation with Susanne about the 'Feminine Principle.' Gabor joined us at some point and contributed his perspective as a male teacher. It was a most delightful and insightful interaction and it was this that inspired me to write this book. Excerpts from this conversation are included in this book.

To watch the entire video with Susanne Marie and several of the conversations with Pierre Richard, please see the Resource page in the front of this book.

I hope that it will have meaning for you too and inspire men and women alike.

> *Many thanks to my dear friends Pierre Richard and Susanne Marie and to my beloved Gabor Harsanyi.*

Chapter One

Oops!

The Most Misunderstood Key

> "Using the mind for the purpose of awakening is like using your GPS system to find a recipe for baking a cake!"

After several years of hard work, Mark finally became a manager at his place of employment - a large international corporation. Although he was thrilled (temporarily) he strived for more. He was extremely ambitious when it came to his career and was eager to climb the corporate ladder no matter what it would take.

He began working longer and longer hours and taking on more and more responsibilities. He went to several courses to upgrade his skills and never missed an opportunity to compliment and suck up to the CEO, Mr. Jacob. He was so focused on his goal, that he made sure not to form any friendships at work that could hinder his achievement or distract him from his objective. He only befriended colleagues who were above his position since they could, he thought, be good influences and help him.

For this reason, he did his best to reject and ignore any of the friendly remarks he often received in the lunch room from a young newcomer by the name of Joseph. Joseph was simple, full of youthful jolly, and inexperienced in the cut-throat corporate environment. For a while he did not even notice Mark's dismissive responses to him. He kept giving him the benefit of the doubt seeing how busy Mark kept himself (or rather made himself appear). Eventually Mark augmented his efforts to push Joseph away by hurling insults and invalidations.

Years went by and Mark was denied every opportunity that came up for a promotion. There were so many times that he could have become a director or even a VP, but each time his entry into those ranks was blocked. This, of course, troubled him tremendously... and rightfully so, as he made all the right efforts (or did he?)

Finally, out of sheer desperation, Mark gathered some chutzpah, swallowed his pride, and requested to meet with Mr. Jacob, the CEO of this large conglomerate. He began to speak about all his hard work and described to Mr. Jacob in great detail all his accomplishments. Mr. Jacob listened with a smile and much patience. When Mark at last gave him a chance to respond, it was not at all what he expected.

"Yes, you have worked very hard. No doubt about that." Said Mr. Jacob. "But your efforts are in vain since you are not a very nice person to be around. Why would we want an intolerant and unfriendly man to be a director or VP?"

"What do you mean?" replied poor Mark trying to hide his shock and block out some uncertain shame. "I made many friends here. All the other managers like me!"

"That may be so, Mark. But my son, Joseph, is very hurt by you. You certainly missed the "mark" with him. Not knowing that Joseph is my son, you have been kissing the wrong butts."

This is how we go through our spiritual journey. We give all our attention to the mind and its conglomerate of mental tools and skills and try to win favor with any teacher who sounds smart and who impresses us. Lord knows, I have done this for years. But there is something else that we ought to engage if we are to get close to the lofty position called 'BEING HOME.' We need to form an alliance with the body.

The body is a replica of the universe. We have all heard the words "As without so within," or the "microcosm and the macrocosm" are the same. Not one doctor, healer or Indian chief knows all the body's secrets and how it works. It is run and operated by none other than the universal intelligence, which we might call God (if that word does not offend us). We have no greater ally than our own body. Making friends with it, going within it, feeling its essence and inner vitality is the key. The body itself is the door or the gateway to our own conscious being. This is the right connection to make in order to unite with the divine universal intelligence.

So, what happened? How did we become so stupid to miss this mark and ignore the closest thing to us... the son or daughter of the universal consciousness we so wish to become?

Well, it's not that we are stupid. We have simply been conned. We have been conned by the very thing we so revere – the mind. There is no greater threat to the mind than the body itself since the mind cannot control it in any meaningful way. When we are in the body and 'feeling' its aliveness, the mind is still... not relaxed, but still! It is no longer in the position of authority.

Not wanting to lose control, the mind, in its cunning, smart and manipulative fashion created religion, spirituality, philosophy, metaphysics and all the rest of the dazzling 'feel good' entertainers out there – all of which are mind-based, and most of which condemn the body in fear of the truth being revealed. It even invented the 'relaxed state of mind' achieved through conventional meditation, so it can continue to prevail by keeping us busy and looking forward to a future accomplishment. This is fine in the mental/intellectual domain, but awakening is not an accomplishment.

Many of my former teachers consistently spewed out phrases like "you are not the body," "the body is the trap," "the body is nothing but a shit factory," etc. It is never wise to use divisive and denouncing phrases in teachings that supposedly promote unity. Many seekers of truth have learned to ignore or even despise the body... except, of course, when beautifying it assists in creating an improved self-image for the mind-based ego.

It is only through activating our body as a transformational organ operated by the universal intelligence that we can ever hope to enter the kingdom of God. As I mentioned in my previous book - *The Blind Leading the Blonde: Confessions of a Recovering Spiritual Junkie* - it was only when Gabor guided me to feel the body within, that I recognized, after 40 long years of seeking, that all my previous spiritual efforts were in the mind. Damn! I was sucking up to the wrong managers! (see Resource page to access this book)

Peace Follows Renunciation... of What?

Throughout the ages we've been hearing of people starving the body of food or pleasures or practicing astral travel in an attempt to leave the body. What we need to leave behind (temporarily at least) is the mind... not the body.

There once was a king in ancient India who had a very hard time dealing with all the responsibilities of being a king due to his overly busy mind. One day he heard a lecture by a visiting monk. The monk's words "Peace follows renunciation!" struck a chord with him, and he became obsessed with this mantra.

After some agitated mental deliberation, he summoned his wife, the queen, and announced to her that he was planning to renounce his throne and go live in the forest as a recluse. He asked her to take over all the responsibilities of the kingdom on his behalf.

The queen was completely unperturbed by this. She was enlightened and was established in the silence of being, even while attending the affairs of the kingdom. She gave her blessing to the king, and off he went with very few and simple pieces of clothes and a meditation mat.

After several months the queen wondered how her husband was doing. She disguised herself as an old sage and went to the forest. When she found him sitting outside his tiny hut, she deepened her voice and said. "How nice to meet a hermit like you meditating here in the forest. What have you achieved so far"?

"Well, not as much as I had expected". Replied the king, not recognizing this visitor. "I have given up my kingdom and now live a very simple life here. I have renounced a life of comfort and luxury. I have relinquished my wife, good food and all kinds of pleasures, as well as responsibilities, duties and concerns. There

THE FEMININE PRINCIPLE: THE KEY TO AWAKENING FOR MEN AND WOMAN

is really nothing here to excite or agitate me. It is very quiet. There is a nice creek nearby and enough berries to survive on. But, somehow my mind is still running, and I can't seem to stop it. I have not been able to find the peace that I so desire."

"Peace follows renunciation!" pronounced the queen imitating the authoritative and resolute voice of a wise sage and then quickly walked away.

The king was stunned that these words showed up again. "What else can I give up"? he thought. "Well, I don't really need my hut. So, what if I will get a bit wet when it rains and hot in the summer. Yes! That shall be my next sacrifice. I will renounce my hut!"

Months went by and the queen came back in her disguise. "I see you have renounced your hut." She said in a deep sage-like tone. "Good for you! How is that working out for you? Found peace now?"

"Not really." Replied the king somewhat embarrassed by his lack of achievement. "What would *you* suggest?"

"Peace follows renunciation!" declared the queen again and once again vanished from sight.

"Oh shit..." sighed the king. "Now what? Oh... I know! I will get rid of the few clothes I have. I don't really need to wear anything here. I'll just have a small piece of cloth around my private parts and that's it. That will surely be a good next step in my renunciation."

More time went by, and sure as shooting, the queen returned to check up on her miserable husband. "Great! I see you are naked now. Another good act of renunciation. How is the peace coming along?"

"Oye... don't ask." Mumbled the king with deep disappointment. "What peace? My mind just won't stop! I am more disturbed than ever."

And once again.... "Peace follows renunciation!" affirmed the queen before her disappearance.

"Not again! Now what? Fine! Whatever! I will stop eating. I don't care anymore. I must find peace. If I have to starve myself then so be it."

Knowing that the king's next step would probably be self-inflicted hunger, the queen returned after a few short days.

"You lost weight." She said as if it was a great discovery. "Good for you! You must have renounced food. Way to go! So? How's the peace? Found it yet?"

"You would think, but no!" replied the emaciated and somewhat delirious king. "There must be another way."

"Peace follows renunciation!" once again asserted the queen and off she went.

"This is ridiculous!" cried the king. "I can't live without peace. I have renounced everything! What is left?" He sat for a while in his dejected and depressed state, and then an idea came to him. "I got it! Since all I have left is this body, it must be the culprit and the cause for all my agonizing attachments and restlessness. I will get rid of the body. Surely I will find peace when my body is destroyed."

With a renewed sense of resolve the king began to gather wood to make a big fire. He then found a couple of sticks and rubbed them together till an ember was created. He used the ember to set the wood on fire and stood by it, preparing himself for his big moment, as the fire grew bigger and taller. The queen, knowing her man, never really left. She was hiding behind a tree. As soon as she saw the king making his move to leap into the fire, she jumped out and grabbed him... still in the disguise of a sage, of course.

"What the are you doing?" she called out in a scolding and 'no longer saintly' manner.

"Why, I am renouncing the last thing I have left." Replied the king both shocked and slightly annoyed at the interference. "I have renounced everything else and still haven't found peace. It must be my body that is causing all this disturbance. Hence, I am about to renounce my body. Please don't stand in my way."

"No, you schmuck." Said the queen in a manly way. "Your body is not - and never was - the irritant. Your mind is. Your body is the doorway to the kingdom of heaven where there is nothing but peace. All you need to do is knock on this door by turning your attention within, and your mind will slow down and become still. There is no need to renounce anything – not even your mind. Once you retrieve your inner throne by going inside, your mind will become your servant and will never bother you again."

As the queen guided him to feel his body from within, the king finally got it. Peace filled his entire being as he returned to the kingdom to rule from a new place of love and pure being.

> *"Peace is not a state of mind. It has nothing to do with being happy or sad, contented or troubled, wealthy or poor, active or inactive."* **Gabor**

The Feeling Mode

We so often feel the need to get out of the city and spend time in a forest, or by the ocean. This recharges us and reduces our stress. We enjoy so much giggling with a baby, playing with a dog, or riding a horse. The trees, the ocean, a baby (still uncorrupted by education), a dog or any animal – all these are directly connected to, intertwined with and completely supported by the universal intelligence. They are not ruled by a mind. *We* are... and therefore, when we need a break from our constant oppressor we long for anything that will connect us to our inner silence, our original being.

However, these wonderful experiences for the most part are still in the mind... a more relaxed 'state of mind'... but the mind nonetheless. On rare occasions, and for some people, the mind becomes so relaxed that one accidently and unknowingly drops into the inner body, and for a few moments consciousness is allowed to arise from within.

> *The same universal consciousness that we seek in nature is very much alive in our bodies as well. Turning our attention within to connect with IT is not the same as a temporary relaxed state of mind.*

In our current dimension/state we operate and make distinctions with our senses - visual, auditory, olfactory, etc. When we look we notice various sizes, shapes, colors and items. Take a moment and notice what's in front of you. The chair you are sitting on looks different from the table next to you, for example. In the same way, when we listen we distinguish between sounds – loud, soft, musical, annoying, etc. This is life as we know it and as we have been accustomed to experiencing. We notice, compare, label and store this information based on our propensities and circumstances. When we go to the forest or play with a dog we are using our outer senses and our minds to create a pseudo natural state.

Waking up from this dimension takes us to a different mode of perception. Here, our most commonly used senses and the interpretations of what they perceive by the mind are no longer relevant. In fact, the mind and senses are not even capable of processing this non-dimension. This is a realm where we use feeling as a distinguishing factor. Being present, going within, being in our body, or any other way we wish to call it (no words are accurate really, since words belong to the duality world... but we try...) – this is the world of feeling. There is a distinct feeling. When it arises from within, it is recognized as HOME.

Thus, when we attempt to connect with the universal intelligence by going within, unlike escaping to a forest or the ocean, we are connecting through feeling rather than through the mind and senses. We can still enjoy these places and experiences with our senses, but when the body has been activated through inner attention, the enjoyment is on a whole other level. Please don't try to understand this with the mind. To know what is being said here, it is imperative to have the shift from the sense world to the realm of silence... or non-sense.

> *"The realm of awakening is a distinct feeling. When it arises from within, it is recognized as HOME."* **Gabor**

The Shift from Spirituality to Awakening

Please note, I am not at all against spirituality. I had been highly spiritual for many years. I had moments of great enthusiasm and ecstasy, but also many of deep depression and disappointment since my search was never fulfilled on the level that I longed for – awakening. Mind-based spirituality can keep us going for a long time, but it is impossible to leap out of duality via the mind. Asking the mind to leap out of its own dualistic foundation would be like asking a teenager to give up texting.

> *Mulla Nasiruddin's Jewish cousin, Schlemiel, was crouching under a street light searching for his lost keys. Several people came by to help him, but to no avail. Finally, Rabbi Goldstein showed up and, having heard about the lost keys, he asked Schlemiel:*
>
> *"Where were you when you dropped your keys?"*
>
> *"Over there!" exclaimed Schlemiel, pointing to an area a few blocks further.*
>
> *"So why are you searching here?" asked the puzzled Rabbi.*
>
> *"Isn't it obvious?" responded Schlemiel with a question.*
>
> *"This is where the light is!"*

Having made the shift from the spirituality of our duality dimension to the silence of being, many of my previously held concepts fell away making space for new clarity to arise. Perhaps one of the most important insights that emerged was that awakening is not just different from spirituality as I knew it, but it is not even in the same realm.

In our duality dimension we learn through our education system to value expansion, achievement, motivation, information, smarts, self-image and everything that belongs to the egoic mind that thrives on contrast and opposites. We enjoy learning, making comparisons, accumulating and amassing knowledge, winning, competing, evaluating, etc. This is what makes our bi-polar world go around. When one has awakened, and consciousness starts to take precedence over our self-created conglomerate of mental concepts and beliefs, our values change.

What more does a royal being need to do to enhance his or her self-image? When we know we are the king or queen, we need not compete or strive for more. When peace is our natural habitat, we no longer chase after the dramatic effects of highs and lows. When we are at HOME, when we are living 'as' the silence of being, the entire game changes, as do the rules of existence.

At first there is an innocent awkwardness since we are not used to this mode of being. The mind, with all the mental templates that it has accumulated over the years of living in duality, tries like hell to regain its control and will feed us any number of lies and doubts to win us back and to, once again, take over our attention.

For this reason, so many spiritual modalities and new age teachings – even those who use phrases such as non-duality, awakening, etc. – have built in them the same type of components - such as learning, thinking, analyzing, comparing, achieving, etc. - as we have grown accustomed to through our education.

Our false sense of security relies heavily on continuity. We become spiritual and yet we want to continue using the same methods and faculties as we have been taught to use in our non-spiritual life. Even when we want to awaken, we often approach this new pursuit as if it were a continuation of all our previous spiritual endeavors. It can't be. We say that spirituality has prepared us for awakening. But how could that be, when awakening is a complete leap out of everything that the mind is familiar with – including spirituality?

As Sammy the butterfly was flying around one fine morning, spreading good cheer and showing off his colorful wings, he noticed a couple of caterpillars repeatedly leaping off a small twig and falling to the ground.

"What are you doing?" he asked them innocently. "Why do you keep on making yourselves tumble like that?"

"A famous caterpillar guru told us that we could become butterflies like you and we will be able to fly." One of the caterpillars began to explain (could have been the male caterpillar... hard to tell). "He said that if we worked hard and kept practicing, we will be well prepared and someday in the future it might happen. We have been doing this for a long time, but we still can't fly. Any advice you can give us?"

"Are you out of your teensy tiny minds?" responded Sammy the butterfly. "There is no way you could fly with those sticky legs, no matter how many of them you have. I was a butterfly like you not too long ago, but I had to go through a complete transformation before I could fly. There is no way you can prepare for it with the apparatus you have now. And by the way, have you ever seen your caterpillar guru fly?"

A butterfly is not a continuation of a caterpillar. It does not resemble a caterpillar in any way shape or form. It is an entirely different mode of existence.

There are teachers and teachings that give lots of information to learn, but no experience. Those teachers often have a persona or an image of someone very mystical, special, or even super-human – dark skin, from a faraway country, wearing special clothes, very charismatic, has long hair, has come from a well-known and long-lived lineage, has many spiritual accolades and diplomas, has had many spiritual experiences since they were a child and on and on.

The teachings are usually based on past information - ancient if possible... the older the better... even though the words 'the now' are thrown in from time to time. They are founded on others' experiences and are filled with future promises which are totally unachievable... yet the rewards are so tantalizing, and so many people follow them, that hardly anyone notices this.

On our second date Gabor and I were having dinner at a restaurant on an outdoor patio. I was mentioning to him that the first teaching that I belonged to had hundreds of thousands of devotees and followers, and how difficult it was to leave when clearly, so many people found this teaching worth following. His response was, "When there is a piece of shit on the ground, millions of flies are drawn to it. A million flies can't all be wrong, can they?" Aha!!!

But I digress... so back to my point – the reason so many teachings don't work is simply because they are mind-based. They adopt the same logic, structure and values of our education system that robs us of the ability to rely on our own direct experience. And worst of all, they are based on the premise that one has to deserve or earn the right to awaken. One must put forth a lot of effort to attain a future prize, and this is all authorized by some mysterious person or dogma. We are so eager to defend our spiritual paths by declaring that they are not a religion, but... excuse me....

... been there, done that, bought the T-shirt! After 40 years of spiritual seeking and practice I knew more about false teachers and teachings than I could ever hope to know about God.

Question:

I am interested in awakening but don't know very much and I think I need to acquire more knowledge on this topic first. Any books or spiritual courses you can recommend?

Gabor:

One of the biggest obstacles to awakening to our original self is bookstores. You walk into any bookstore and under New Age or Self Help you will literally find thousands of books. So, we get a clear impression that all or most of the knowledge in those books is necessary for our awakening or even for bettering our life. You might find in bookstores some good tips for making your life better intellectually, not knowing that awakening itself, which is a solution to all life's problems, is not found in books.

As a matter of fact, the over use of intellect through books or spiritual courses is one of the biggest obstacles to awakening, as is accumulating more and more information about it. Using your intellect to find anything else about awakening is like moving the filth in a pigpen from one corner to another without realizing you are still in the pigpen. It is much better to step out of the pigpen altogether.

Chapter Two

Reviving the Feminine Principle

"Me Too"

> *"The unifying instrument for all existence – although it is 'within' us - has been atrophied. It must be re-activated, if humanity is to get back to its origin."* **Gabor**

Another area where the realm of duality, the domain of the mind, has seeped into spirituality is the male dominance in the age-long masculine-feminine power struggle. On a mundane level – and I boldly include religion in this! - it is a known fact that women have been suppressed, excluded, looked down upon, persecuted, sexually abused and even tortured or killed for many centuries. I am sure many volumes of research have been written on this, relaying accounts from many cultures around the globe. So, I need not pour more oil on that fire by adding more horror stories.

Sure, in the Western world there have been some improvements... women can finally vote! Yay!!! Meanwhile in Sudan, it is legal for 10-year old girls to be forced into marriage and to be repeatedly raped by their husbands. So, let us not fool ourselves. After so many decades and centuries of ongoing abuse worldwide, the emotional charge swept under carpets and stowed away in our collective global psyche is not going to just "poof" away, just because women can now vote, hold a position as CEO or even a president of a country in some more 'advanced' cultures.

The "Me Too" movement has not sprung up with such momentum merely due to recent events exposed by some famous movie stars. This is a long time coming and I hope it gains enough power to influence women's rights in third world countries as well.

In my youth I had at least four near-rape and sexual harassment experiences that I can remember. In those days no one did or said anything about that. Nowadays, we've gone to the other extreme. If a boss sneezes the wrong way, he is accused of sextual harassment.

Not too long ago, while still in the corporate world in Toronto, I was sitting in the lunch room with a few other managers. I began telling them about the successful training program I just did at the head office in New Jersey, and how moved I was by the appreciation of the owner/CEO of the company.

"As my cab was pulling out of the company's parking lot to take me to the airport, the owner ran after the cab and waved it to stop. He then opened the taxi door where I was sitting, and as I got out to see what he wanted, he gave me a big hug and thanked me for training his sales staff."

"What?" exclaimed one very perturbed, male-looking, female manager. "That is NOT ok. You must report him to HR and file an allegation against him. You can sue him! This is a clear case of harassment!"

I couldn't believe my ears! "Why?" I asked, totally baffled by her comment. "He was happy with the results and was expressing his gratitude. In fact, I hugged him back. I was so touched that he would leave his office and run after my cab just to thank me."

This is how things go in the duality reality we live in. There is a constant swing. From being victimized and oppressed we swing to extreme and, at times, unrealistic intolerance.

And so, now it seems as though the abscess of cruelty to women is about to burst. The good news is that there is a clear and unifying solution and resolution to all this, which is what is motivating me to write this book. So please read on. And, no, I will not be needing to join the "Me Too" movement.

The spiritual arena has not been spared. Here too we find the infiltration of feminine degradation. In the early years of my spiritual search I never heard of a female spiritual teacher. Male teachers had little to no respect for female teachers for a long time. It was later on that I became aware of several female teachers that had sprung forth, but not without exerting a substantial amount of misguided personal power to sustain their positions. Having had to fight for power and to struggle to be heard for so long, here too, on the spiritual battle field, it has become much the same.

Before my first teacher passed away, he appointed two successors – a brother and a sister. Shortly after his death, a huge conflict burst out between these supposedly enlightened siblings. Not being established in BEING, the sister took over by unleashing all her suppressed personal power and emasculating her brother. Like me, most people followed the sister since she appeared more powerful. I tried for six years to adjust to her, but never succeeded. Her over-compensation for being a female turned her into a power-hungry masculine-like teacher.

My next teacher (male) spoke very poorly of women and went as far as declaring that only a man can be a true master. In the spiritual group that he founded, the women did most of the work, yet whenever a man left the group, there was always a blaming finger pointing at a woman. Being treated as second class citizens in this organization and having no permission to express their frustration, the women soon began to emasculate the men. Once again, the women were scolded for castrating the men who were now reduced to feeble weaklings.

It's a Set-up

Language and education have truly distorted our outlook on gender and have wreaked havoc in the male/female relationship by promoting masculine supremacy from the so-called beginning of time.

We are taught in school at a very young age about Adam and Eve. God made Adam first and then... oops... a man by himself cannot procreate. What to do? What to do? Alrighty then... let's create another human with a womb. And so, a 'wom(b)man' was created... perhaps as an afterthought (who knows?).

And then came the big scandal – Eve, the **woman,** got conned by a snake (metaphor for the mind, perhaps??) and broke the law. There was only one law back in those good old days, unlike today where we have more laws than China has rice. And yet she – a woman – broke it. TMZ could have had a field day with that scandal. But alas, there was no population yet that could be dazzled by this gossip.

Nonetheless, the story got around throughout the ages and every little boy and girl eventually get to find out all about the wrong doing of the first woman (the real first lady) and why women deserved to be punished and were made to suffer by none other than the angry and unforgiving supreme judge – Yup! God himself! Ouch!

Really? Are we still buying this? Personally, I wasn't there, so I don't really know, but what I do know from my own experience is that we have been taught to believe whatever the "grown-ups" tell us – parents, teachers, books, doctors, professors – you know... the big people with overly developed minds and education.

And then, of course, all the above is nailed down via language. In Hebrew, one of the most ancient languages, the word for wife is 'woman' and the word for husband is 'owner'. So, a man calls his wife 'my woman', and a woman calls her husband 'my owner'.

Sounds a bit bitchy to me. Still wonder how masculine dominance came about?

I am not here to judge anyone's beliefs. I can't blame anyone for accepting a theory that has been ingrained into our collective psyche for centuries. It's a sticky one for sure. However, some do hope for emancipation from the historical stories and have gone through the trouble of doing all kinds of research.

BREAKING NEWS!

Jesus was not the only one who was conceived immaculately!

According to author Drunvalo Melchizedek, there is now hard evidence that immaculate conception is not only true, but it is part of everyday life. In other words, although a man can't procreate without a woman, a woman can, and has throughout history, been able to give birth without any participation by a man. Take that Adam! Jesus was not the only one who was conceived immaculately. Apparently, there were many others, and this has been found to be true not only with humans, but also in other forms of nature.

For example, a female bee can give birth to a male bee any time she wants, with no involvement of a male partner. She only needs a partner to give birth to a female bee. As a result of this, the procreation of bees creates a family tree that expands in a Fibonacci sequence. This is explained in great detail and with much clarity in Drunvalo's book *The Ancient Secret of the Flower of Life, Volume Two*.

So, you tell me, which came first? The chicken or the egg? Adam or Eve? Did God really need to knock Adam out, take out one of his ribs and create a whole new gender? Could he not have simply created Eve first knowing well that she could give birth to a man on her own?

Perhaps the entire story of creation is one big misunderstood and misinterpreted assortment of metaphors. Maybe at some point in time, it all made perfect sense... until it trickled down from one unconscious mind to another, as its deep meaning slowly but surely faded away. And now, all we have left is a 'who done it' with a finger pointing at the female.

Like I said, I wasn't there, and I am certainly no scholar. Who am I to say what really happened. And in the higher scheme of non-things, what does it really matter? Nonetheless, I feel it is high time to start questioning the concepts, the stories and the lies we are fed. Especially those that cause separateness and divisiveness, and those that promote fear, guilt and shame.

Not in order to become smarter, but for the sole purpose of freeing ourselves of the conflicting mess that we are in and the never-ending battle of the sexes. I am not much into conspiracy theories, but it sure feels as though humanity has fallen victim to a divide and conquer type of manipulation. We need not put up with this any longer.

"Men Are from Mars Women from Venus" - Useful or Not?

At some point a slight diversion emerged to bridge the separation gap. A wave arose of semi-spiritual books and blogs offering comfort and support (or was it a feeble cover-up??). The intent was to shed light on - or should I say, present a more 'modern way' of viewing - the differences between men and women. It did not address the root problem, but it assisted to some degree by fostering understanding between the sexes. It was a good start and a very necessary one to prevent married people from killing each other.

Unfortunately, as in most issues belonging to this duality existence (including spirituality!), an equal amount (perhaps even more) of confusing books and blogs have sprung up, spewing a gazillion and one made-up theories explaining, dissecting, analyzing, making excuses, creating false concepts and downright bullshitting about this topic. I am not going to get into that here since that is not the objective of this book. My intent here is to bring a more unifying perspective from my discovery and experience of a realm that transcends separation, including the difference between genders.

During my 'spiritual' days I have experienced plenty of maltreatment and suppression on an emotional level in my first marriage. After my divorce I wanted so much to remain single in order to avoid the gender struggle, the abuse and the heartache that goes with it. I promised myself I will never be in a relationship again. I lasted 18 years as a single woman... till I met Gabor. I will write about my current conscious relationship with him later on in this book, since it has to do with the unifying solution I mentioned earlier. Relationships are not going away. They have a very important purpose.

> *"A relationship is the best ongoing seminar for the Western mind. It provides an integral part of the practices that we do, since it would be difficult to perturb you as much in a seminar, as it would with a partner."* **Gabor**

From my video "The Female Principle: An Evolutionary Necessity"

I recently had a video conversation with my dear friend Susanne Marie, who is a spiritual mentor and the founder of *Susanne Marie – The World as Yourself*, about this matter. Here is an excerpt of Susanne's words:

> "Denying the feminine in the expression of women and in the expression of mother earth and the feminine with all of us actually, is what is creating such a hostile environment for the planet... for all people to be able to survive. The way we treat the feminine is our own denial of life. We have such a skewed conditioned way of seeing and relating to the body, to form, and to the expressions that we have called feminine. It's not any one gender's fault, it's just that it is really such an important time to look at all of this behavior and bring it to the light.

> "In the spiritual arena it is the same kind of thing. Women teachers are not deemed in the same esteem. And they can be saying the same things or even more profound things, but it is not valued in the same kind of way (as male teachers). And this has been throughout time... thousands of years.

> "Of course, there are times and periods and maybe individual female teachers who have been viewed with esteem. I am not saying that that doesn't even occur now. And there are plenty of men who are not operating with this kind of patriarchal system. However, it is so deeply ingrained within us all – including the women!

> "For me, coming out as a teacher, initially, was really to go against this kind of inner silencing of my own knowing... my own voice. Part of my growth and continued growth has been

to un-silence myself and to give permission to this 'knowing that we are' to have a voice! To speak truth and to not apologize for what I know.

"I work with men and women and I have a women's group. And these are wise and empowered women who still shake when they are asked to speak truth. It is so programmed, and we are looking at this as a group. I invite us all to look at where it is that we are silencing the feminine."

"Part of my growth and continued growth has been to un-silence myself and to give permission to this 'knowing that we are' to have a voice!" **Susanne Marie**

Now Let's Leap Beyond Gender, Shall We!

There is a whole other level where this needs to change. This brings us back to the difference between mind-based spirituality and true awakening. Please note, I am no longer talking about gender here. This has to do with the masculine-like and feminine-like approaches to teachings and the various modalities.

Systematized teachings, structured meditations, jnana yoga, knowledge-based traditions, teachings that focus on understanding, interpretations, explanations, comparisons and research – all these are masculine types of teachings. They have been mostly taught by men for many centuries and have mostly come from far away exotic lands. This, of course, has made them seem highly credible. Thus, they have become readily accepted and deeply rooted in spiritual communities.

Furthermore, the fact that the masculine types of teachings involve the mind has contributed greatly to its popularity. Most people prefer them since anything to do with the mind wins – it's our comfort zone.

The feminine approach has to do more with surrender, being, heart, feeling, humility... or as Susanne Marie so beautifully put it in our conversation:

"It's not a doing... it's feeling, being, sensing, leaning back and letting go, instead of leaning forward and doing, and striving and seeking, wanting to conquer... the mind wanting to conquer and take control – those are not popular, but it is what the world needs."

At one point, Gabor joined my conversation with Susanne, and here is what he added to our conversation:

"There is a distinction that must be made, without which,

awakening will not happen. In my experience, while going through the eye of the needle (as a metaphor for leaping beyond this dimension) as in awakening, or in an initiation, we cannot take across any explanation, gathered up information, history, etc. We must be totally naked to actually go through. We must completely surrender and be totally in this wonderful feminine type of space. At this stage we've gone beyond gender but, since we are using duality language, I refer to this approach as 'feminine-like.'

"In my experience that kind of initiation happens between a teacher and a student, person to person. It happens orally in a 'moment-to-moment' kind of conversation and experience. It is the 'moment-to-moment'ness that helps the student go through the eye of the needle. And that 'moment-to-moment'ness is absolutely a 'feminine-like' energy. There is no way we can give birth to this kind of consciousness without the feminine energy.

"Since language is in duality, 'moment-to-moment'ness is the best term I can use when referring to the timelessness of BEING… which, to the mind that is still in duality, is observed as the NOW in each moment." **Gabor**

"We can have 100 or 200 male types of meditation, explanations, information gathering, and all kinds of interesting things. We can have hundreds of structured meditations. When push comes to shove, at the end, it must be this utter surrendered, naked, wonderful, loving female type of energy.

"In the last stages of learning, in other words, going through the eye of the needle or actually BEING 'there' and actually being able to stay 'there', it is absolutely essential to have this 'moment-to-moment'ness.

"In a male dominated structured society, I think that the structured kind of meditation is more popular. Therefore, that may give rise to the fact that male teachers are more popular. It's more structured, it's more interesting… we can bring up

more history, we can bring up more mystery, we can structure, structure, structure...

"When it comes to actually BEING there, we have to be totally naked and we can't bring anything across. It is my opinion, that's what is missing from initiations and from awakenings is this last piece of 'moment-to-moment'ness type of learning, where the teaching is person to person, moment to moment which, as I said, is entirely feminine-like.

"Now what I can predict is that the preference for male teachers will shift to female teachers. More and more people are starting to realize that this last segment to awakening comes much more naturally to females than to males. The more people realize that, the more popular female teachers are going to be. It comes more naturally to a female to be in 'moment to moment'ness and in feeling. God is a feeling. God is not an explanation. It is not a structure. It is a heart-related feeling.

"Most of the work I do is in the feminine mode. I do that last component, where people go through and stay there. When I have to do a lot of explanation, it feels to me as if I am wrestling with somebody. So, I go to the feminine mode even though I am a man.

"In this male dominated society, eventually, if we don't actually focus on our heart and feeling, we are not going to make it. It's not just a conversation any more... it is an emergency! Really! I don't want to scare people, but without human awakening, we are really screwed. My experience is that 'spirituality' has been mainly riding on this level of past and future kind of a mind-based structure.

"So, there is a male dominated mind-based structure and spirituality came around and put all the good spiritual knowledge on top of the male dominated structure-oriented stuff. And now we have a whole bunch of spiritual knowledge in the context of male dominance structure and there is no room in it. Spirituality became very popular. The mind loves exercises in which, "I am going to start here, and I am going to

get somewhere." The mind loves this. So, if I come up with any kind of special technique in which in six months from now you are going to get somewhere, it's going to be very popular.

"On the other hand, if I say, "Look, you can only enter the NOW now. There is the technology available to enter the NOW now, and the only thing that takes time is the integration" - the mind hates that, because we go beyond the mind immediately.

"Currently, spirituality is mainly on the horizontal time-based level packed with all kinds of goodies. Awakening is stepping out of time. Stepping out of time is 90% feminine. This must become much more popular than it currently is. My recommendation is that female teachers focus on the feminine teachings that step out of time. Why bother with the horizontal male teachings? It's not there anyway! Without the jumping out of the male mode to the female mode we are not going to get anywhere. So why not specialize in this 'moment-to-moment'ness and emphasize that.

"Perhaps by being more vocal about it, and more deliberate about it, that approach can be a lot more popular and conducive to awakening and for society to survive."

"In this male dominated society, eventually, if we don't actually focus on our heart and feeling, we are not going to make it. It's not just a conversation any more... it is an emergency!" **Gabor**

No Gender has Monopoly on Being an Awakening Teacher

The following riddle was run by two groups - 197 BU psychology students and 103 children, ages 7 to 17, from Brookline summer camps:

"A father and son are in a horrible car crash that kills the dad. The son is rushed to the hospital; just as he's about to go under the knife, the surgeon says, 'I can't operate—that boy is my son!' Explain."

The researchers who conducted this experiment found that even young people and self-described feminists tended to overlook the possibility that the surgeon in the riddle was a 'she.' Only 14 percent of the students and 15 percent of the children (yay kids!) got the answer right – "The surgeon was the boy's mother."

Oddly enough, in the BU student group the women outnumbered the men two-to-one, and it included mothers who were employed or were doctors... and yet, they had so much difficulty with this riddle. Many of the BU students theorized: the son had two gay fathers, or the "father" in the car referred to a priest, or the surgeon was "horribly confused," or, the whole scenario was a dream as we see on TV shows. The children had more imaginative answers such as - the surgeon was a robot, or a ghost, or "the dad laid down and officials thought he was dead, but he was alive."

If we are so conditioned and confused about a surgeon being male or female, is it any wonder that the same thing goes on with respect to spiritual teachers?

We will probably never succeed in eliminating gender prejudice and the battle of the sexes through mind-based spirituality. As long as we are governed by duality, we will continue to remain captive under the rule of conflicting forces and oppositions. This is why leaping out of duality and out of the mind's grip through true awakening is not only essential at this time, but it is also the only solution we have at our disposal.

By 'awakening' I do not mean waking up to the realization that we have been manipulated, educated incorrectly, misguided by our parents and society as a whole or fooled by religions, dogmas and false beliefs. That would just be waking up from one dream to another. I am talking about a complete and radical leap out of this mind-dominated dimension and entering our inner kingdom as the natural, simple and pristine BEING that we are in essence.

> *"Awakening is the ability to 'bypass' the mind's participation when necessary. It is the moment when Being is recognizing itself."* **Gabor**

A teacher who is truly awakened is not living in duality and, therefore, is beyond gender. At this point, it matters not if the teacher is male or female. He or she can guide initiates via the feminine-like type of approach of humility, surrender and being, with no intellectual entanglements and with no conflict of gender. If one is genuine in his or her quest for true awakening, the criteria for choosing or accepting an awakening teacher should have nothing to do with the teacher's gender.

The Monk and the Prostitute

There once was a very devout and disciplined monk who lived in a small apartment in a rundown neighborhood of a crowded city in India. In the same building, just across the hall from him, lived a prostitute. Every day they saw each other coming or going, but they never talked, as they had little in common.

Whenever the prostitute saw the monk, she was filled with awe and reverence. She was not proud of the life she was forced to live. Seeing him triggered within her a sense of meekness and humility. "Wow!" she would internally marvel at his sight. "That radiant monk must be so holy, peaceful and wise. I am so fortunate to be able to get a glimpse of his presence now and again."

The monk had quite a different reaction upon seeing the prostitute. To him she was a lowly and disgusting creature who did not deserve any of his attention. He made sure to never make eye contact with her. "Oh, that whore!" he would mumble to himself. "How dare she live in the same building. I am a highly spiritual monk and should be surrounded by pure and pious people... not by this slut. Look at all the men who go in and out of her apartment. Has she no shame.?! How dare she contaminate the atmosphere around me with her filthy presence." So much for not giving her his attention, hey?

Anyhow... as it so happened, one day a great fire broke out and the entire building burned down, killing both monk and prostitute. I guess fire knows no discrimination. It burns whatever is there, no questions asked.

When the monk and the prostitute arrived at the pearly gates, the prostitute was immediately ushered through the gates of heaven. Upon seeing this, the monk was deeply annoyed. So, you can imagine how shocked and outraged he was when he himself was escorted in the direction of hell. "What is going on??!!" he cried, approaching one of the guards as he pulled back. "This is a terrible error. I demand to speak with your supervisor!"

Rolling his eyes as in "here we go again," the poor guard took the monk to speak with the supreme judge. When the monk finally finished his rant, the judge calmly responded:

"Look here your holiness (not!), you may have been wearing the robes of a monk, sitting in meditation and prayers for hours a day, fasting every now and then in keeping with the scriptures' demands, and teaching others how to be spiritual. But your mind was as filthy as the thoughts you were harboring about that beautiful soul whom you called a dirty whore.

"While you were consumed by her sinful nature, she found peace and love whenever she noticed you. She saw in you the embodied presence of God. This filled her entire being with tremendous modesty, veneration, and inner silence. It is her spiritual nakedness that is allowing her to go through the narrow gates of heaven. She considered you enlightened but you were really just entitled. You were nothing but an arrogant pompous ass throwing the weight of your spiritual ego around. It is this heavy weight that is preventing you from getting through."

> *"To go through the gate of awakening we must be naked and free of all spiritual concepts and accomplishments. It is the feminine-like type of surrender, humility and allowing that grants us entry."* **Gabor**

Chapter Three

10 Non-Commandments from Queen "Be"

A Note to Men

Dear men,

When you see the words 'queen'
or 'Queendom' in this book,
please don't feel excluded. This is
for you too.

This is not meant to be sexist or
divisive. In the context of this
book, these phrases have nothing
to do with gender!

They are used in reference to the
inner kingdom that is feminine-
LIKE in nature.

It is this feminine-LIKE quality
that restores the balance and
allows us to reclaim our throne.

1. Dear Women, No Need to be Like Men

In the age-long struggle that women have endured, many have tried to assert themselves by attempting to be more masculine. Women have endeavored to be strong, powerful, success-oriented, intellectual, decisive, abrupt, harsh, in control, assertive, assured, confident, aggressive, etc. There is nothing wrong with all those qualities or traits in themselves. However, if they are sought after due to an egoic need to compete with men, to be like men or as a solution for overcoming suppression – that will never work. It is never wise to invite or create any changes from that place of conflict.

This tendency makes women less attractive and it confuses the hell out of men. They don't know what reaction they will get if they open a door for a woman or stand up when she enters a room. Why give up these beautiful feminine perks?

On a mundane level, women are not men. They are different – not better, not worse, not even opposite – just different. This is the domain of distinctions, diversity and uniqueness. It is natural and simply the way it is. A male peacock has a magnificent array of colors and is absolutely stunning upon spreading its feathers. The female peacock is pure white. As far as I know, this doesn't seem to bother her. I have not seen or heard of a female peacock trying to paint her feathers.

No matter how much a woman works out, her body is not designed to lift heavy furniture, nor does she have to if she uses her feminine charm and is humble enough to ask for help. No matter how nurturing a man is, he will never be able to give birth. Don't let Arnold Schwarzenegger's movie *Junior* fool you.

In my current marriage to Gabor, although we physically represent different genders, we are equal partners with equal rights - he leaves the toilet seat up, and I leave it down!

2. Dear Women, Find Your Own Power

A woman can be just as successful, powerful and accomplished as a man in her own right. However, for a woman to strive for achievement in order to prove that she is just as qualified as a man is not necessary at all. To be on an equal footing it would be much wiser to acknowledge this polarized existence while dwelling in the only place where unity, sameness and harmony exist – the inner realm of being. If she wants to be strong and powerful, that's where she can find her own true strength, power and confidence.

> *"Confidence that comes from achievement or acquisition is short lived. It will collapse at the first sign of inevitable failure or loss."* **Gabor**

My first husband was born in Yemen and had very strong Middle Eastern male principles. He believed that a woman should listen to and obey her husband no matter what. When I was not in a total surrender mode to his opinions and demands, he would scold me and say, "You have to attune yourself to me!" This made me so mad, but in my habitual suppressed fashion I would find false comfort by inwardly saying to myself, "I want to be attuned to God... not to you, ass-hole!"

One day, out of sheer desperation I went to have an angel reading by a lovely woman who could communicate with angels and seek their help. She had been assaulted by a man and, at a near death moment during the attack, she could suddenly hear angels guiding her to a miraculous escape. From that day, the angels never left her. And so, I decided to see if she could ask them for a solution to my problem with my husband.

After going on and on and spilling my guts about my oppressive husband, she said something that shocked me to the core. "Why are you blaming him? You gave him all your power. Take it back."

"WHAT???!!!!" I spattered in silent despair, trying to fake an agreeable smile, as forbidden anger began to creep in. "I did what????!!!! How could she say that? Is she telling me that it is my fault? Really? *I* am responsible for this? *I* created this? Why would I do that? Even if that were true, how the hell do I get my power back? What is my power anyway?"

Of course, that angel lady was right and deep inside I knew that. I eventually began to see the various ways I was avoiding making decisions and taking responsibility... how I was preventing my own independence by attempting to put my non-existent faith in a man. I didn't know how to be, how to make choices, how to escape blame or shame. So, yes, I gave my power to a man.

For years I struggled and wondered how to get my power and confidence back (as if it could be really 'mine'). I tried to be more assertive and independent. I became an organizer and a leader within the spiritual group I belonged to and taught structured intellectual classes.

When that was over, I pursued a powerful position at work. I was becoming more and more male-like in my nature and behavior... to the point where even when I changed my mind about being single and wanted to find a partner, I was no longer attractive in a feminine way. My attempt to find a man was in a consistent push-pull mode – attract and resist, like and dislike, move forward and escape.

It was only when I met Gabor, who was such a non-threat to my condition, that things began to change. Although I didn't have the means or wherewithal to articulate this back then - and bear in mind I was not yet in love with him – I sensed that Gabor exuded a perfect balance of male-female energy. He was a great listener, compassionate, non-judgmental, kind, allowing, accepting, humble – all of which are feminine-like qualities, and at the same time he was no push over. He was strong, wise, resolute, direct, confident, rational, possessing a clear intellect – all of which are masculine-like qualities.

As I wrote in my book *The Blind Leading the Blonde: Confessions of a Recovering Spiritual Junkie*, it took me two and a half years to actually be able to be with Gabor after meeting him, even though he exuded all of the male and female qualities mentioned above. I was only able to recognize this upon willing to surrender my mind with its screwed-up concepts and templates. . It happened when I was on my way to meet Gabor for our first date after the two-and-a-half-year interval. Here is the section from my book that tells this tale:

On the way to our meeting place a remarkable thing happened that changed my life forever. It was actually the most "undoing" thing I had ever done up until that point, and yet it was indeed most fruitful and rewarding on all levels of existence.

As I began to drive, it suddenly dawned on me that maybe, just maybe, the reason my previous attempts to be with Gabor had failed was because I kept judging him. Looking back, I want to holler, "Ya think?"

"If it is my mind that is holding me back from being with him, I better stop it somehow," I said to myself. "Here is a man with whom I have had several deep and illuminating encounters, yet my mind became agitated, disturbed and filled with resistance instead of letting go of its identity and of the image it had of being a highly spiritual and knowledgeable person."

This shocking observation was a cosmic smack in the face. I immediately stopped the car at a nearby parking lot. I sat quietly for 10 minutes or so and began to release all thoughts. I looked for a place of feeling inside me as opposed to thinking. I stayed with this thought-free stillness for as long as I could. Little did I realize that this was the beginning of a 90-degree shift. Not a 180-degree, which is merely the exchange of bad thoughts for their opposites – good thoughts. This was an act, or non-act, rather, of leaving thoughts behind altogether and transcending them entirely.

Without knowing what was happening I was getting a glimpse of this type of transformation. I was now ready to make the most important decision of my entire life, the solid commitment to myself that when I met Gabor I would remain without any thought, critical or otherwise. I was determined to just be, watch, feel and allow things to occur without the slightest mental interference on my part. With this resolution in my heart I left the parking lot and went to meet Gabor.

Well, what transpired that evening was pure magic. I shall never forget it. There was the embrace from my dreams manifesting in all its unmistakable glory. Amazing! Such profound peace. Unquestionable and unparalleled stillness. And all it took was the conscious decision to suspend thoughts, concepts, analysis and the "oh, so spiritual" identity. Did I mention that this was the best decision I have ever made in my life?

What I was searching for was finally right in front of me and it was only the fucked-up mind that was concealing this fact from me. Go figure! This is the real secret of manifesting that they don't tell you in The Secret or in most law of attraction books and seminars: letting go of your lists of desired outcomes, situations and conditions but even more importantly, not using your mental apparatus for the purpose of co-creating. It interferes every time. (see Resource page to access Nurit's book)

> *I was trying so hard to be powerful in a masculine way when all the while, my true power was buried beneath my suppressed feminine nature.*

I now finally found the kind of power that comes from within and this gives me a new sense of confidence... the confidence to lean back and be as I am. This is the only place to find security since it is unchanging.

3. Dear Women, Beware of Blame

One of the greatest lessons I had to learn after getting my own power back was to watch out for the tendency to blame. It was great to come to the point where I could acknowledge that I was responsible for giving my power away, however, the mind has a sticky nature. Even when it recognizes the truth of something and seemingly goes along with the new 'breakthrough', it still wants to go back and defend its position by finding fault with the oppressor and by spewing blame. It just can't help itself.

It will try to slip and slide away from taking ALL the responsibility whenever it can. "Yes, I gave my power to that man, but he was so controlling and powerful, what could I do?" Says the mind. And here comes one of its favorite 'back-out' strategy phrases: "After all, it takes two to tango." As soon as we say that, we are not taking full responsibility.

There are other ways for us to feel better about ourselves than blaming the other party, in this case the opposite sex. But when we live in our minds, this is what happens. All of a sudden, all men are viewed as pigs or ass-holes who have no respect for women. I can assure you not all men are rapists and I have met countless men who are great supporters of women.

The mind is in duality and it is in constant swing – from good to bad and back again. In the same way, if women are not watchful and if they allow the mind to run their lives - when they regain their power, they can easily swing the other way through blame and be filled with hatred and revenge. The minute we blame we become a victim once again.

I was watching the news this morning as they were showing the conviction of Bill Cosby. It was fascinating to see the expressions on the faces of the women in the various shots that were shown. Some looked relieved, empowered and ready to face the world with renewed confidence, and yet others were filled with anger and thirst for revenge. Revenge is a very satisfying emotion, but it is not at all a useful one. There are plenty of wonderful TV shows (probably most of them) that offer great scenes of revenge, and we can easily experience revenge vicariously by watching them.

> *I was trying so hard to be powerful in a masculine way when all the while, my true power was buried beneath my suppressed feminine nature.*

It is much more productive and elevating to rejoice in our feminine nature and use that power to do what women do best - nurture, create, relax into being, surrender to the flow of the universe, etc.

4. Dear Women, Use Your Pain

The pain we are carrying is not only ours. For all I know we could be schlepping generational, global or even ancestral sisterhood pain. Believe it or not, this can be a great blessing if seen correctly. When we learn to view pain as an ally, as opposed to a foe, our life transforms radically. They say there is no greater pain than labor pain. It certainly proved to be true for me. Yet a woman has the capacity to endure this pain and because of that, a new life can emerge, and we call it a miracle.

In several parts of his book *Functional Silence: De-mystifying Awakening for the Spiritually Exhausted* (and I don't think anyone is more spiritually exhausted than the fair sex!), Gabor talks about the value of pain and suffering. He writes about how to use it as a catalyst, allowing it to propel us into going deep within and resting in our authentic home. Gabor's book is for advanced students of awakening, for people who are willing to read it several times, and/or for anyone who can get past page 50, where a few diagrams are presented. (See Resources page to access this book).

> *"Don't try to fix the catalyst!*
> *It is your best friend."* **Gabor**

It is pain that brings us to our knees. It is pain that wakes us up from the nightmare of dualistic existence and sets us on a permanent platform of lasting peace. Let's face it - no one likes to wake up from a pleasant dream. It was the pain of depression that brought about the great awakenings of teachers like Eckhart Tolle, Gabor Harsanyi and many others.

When I was in India I used to read the beautiful words of female poet-saints. Most were poor, exiled, maimed, raped, poisoned and beaten by their husbands (owners) and even by Brahmin priests, but their words were enlightening and most elevating. Their poetry was filled with such love for God, the divine, and such devotion to truth that one couldn't help but be inspired by reading them. Many of these women started out with horrific life situations, but by allowing pain to open their hearts, they gained tremendous respect and were beloved by truth seeker even after their deaths.

One of these poets was Mirabai. She lived in India in the sixteenth century. She came from royalty, but her unconventional ways and desire to unite with God caused people to ridicule her. Worst of all, her jealous and possessive husband consistently accused her of having an affair, and so he continuously tortured her. He tried so many times to kill her by sending snakes to her room or poisoning her food, but miracles always followed her. The more she suffered, the stronger became her love for God.

> *"Sleep has not visited me the whole night.*
> *Will the dawn ever come?*
> *O my companion! Once I awoke with a start from a dream!*
> *Now the remembrance from that vision never fades.*
> *My life is ebbing as I choke and sigh.*
> *When will the Lord of the afflicted come?*
> *I have lost my senses and gone mad,*
> *But the Lord knows my secret.*
> *He who deals out life and death knows the secret*
> *of Mira's pain."* **Mirabai**

Why let a good calamity go to waste? Would it not be so much wiser to use it to achieve the best possible gift? There is no end to the miracles that take place when we shift our attitude about pain. Gabor and I have seen this time and again with our students, whether they show up with sickness, a troubled relationship or any other life-threatening problem.

5. Dear Woman, Free Your Pain

We are not taught how to deal with emotional pain and certainly not how to free it. Our pain does not necessarily want to stick around and torture us. It's just that we hang on to it with a mind that likes to feed on emotions... especially those it considers to be negative. When we have physical pain like a headache we take a pain killer and it is gone. Many people deal with emotional pain much the same way by turning to alcohol and drugs.

I started out that way prior to becoming spiritual. In my army days in Gaza, I drank a bottle of vermouth every night to escape my mind's alternating painful states of boredom and horror. In my hippie days that followed my release from the army, I got high on drugs. What a great escape that was from the pain of a confused identity!

When I became 'spiritual' I could no longer afford to tarnish my spiritual image by drinking or taking drugs. My new way of avoiding pain became extreme 'busyness' – busyness in the name of service and interpreted as devotion. I worked so hard I had no time to think or feel, and when evening came, I was out like a light. My biggest fear was not having enough things 'to do'. I just dreaded the emptiness of nothing to do. God forbid I should just sit and BE!

The teachings I belonged to for the longest time encouraged busyness and lots of activities. I guess no one knew how else to escape a busy mind. For those who were not inclined to work hard and preferred to appear relaxed and meditative, there was always a mantra that they could repeat incessantly, or hours of chanting. That too kept the mind from delving into stored up pain. And, of course, we were never to show any emotional distress. We were always expected to have that phony blissful smile on our spiritual faces. Oh... the good old days!

By the time I got to Gabor and learned to still the mind internally, I was filled with a tremendous amount of suppressed emotional pain. I was like a ticking time bomb that could destroy a whole city if released at once. Fortunately, when we enter the body and give ourselves to the universal intelligence, there is no sudden and dangerous eruption. This is why we need not 'work on ourselves' when we awaken. We need not plan or toil over our recovery. We can simply allow the universe to do her thing and release the stored-up pain as she sees fit.

This is what started to happen for me. This was my dark night of the soul. The emotional baggage was being released. I don't know what I would have done if Gabor hadn't been there to guide me through this phase. The outbursts of pain, the sobbing, the self-loathing, the insecurities, the depression, the lack of motivation, the desire to no longer exist, the fear and anxiety, the guilt and shame – you name it... it was all there waiting like a lost friend to be recognized, acknowledged and let go.

The odd thing is that I didn't recognize many of the emotions and tendencies that showed up as my own. I eventually learned that some were from the collective generational female pain since, as painful as those emotions were, it was obvious that they had nothing to do with this lifetime of mine.

Other emotions came from my mother. At times it felt as though I was re-living my mother's agony. She suffered a lot due to my father's infidelity when I was young, and she used to come into my bed at night and sob for hours. All this was now coming out. I would sob uncontrollably as if I were in her shoes, even though I was now with Gabor, the most loving and caring man I have ever met.

Gabor explained to me that being a woman, a lot of the pain that women have gone through over the ages, including my mothers and other ancestors, was trying to find their way to freedom through me. He also taught me how to assist the pain and relieve myself from suffering in the midst of it.

He showed me how to feel the pain within my body and allow

myself to just be with it without trying to fix it, ignore it, or even want to get rid of it. Just BE with it... consciously... present. I could rock it like a baby and love it as a long-lost friend and this would free it for good, as long as I held no expectation.

I was now also able to use the pain that was coming up as a motivator to go deeper within. Once one awakens and feels the peace, there is really no more spiritual drive and not much motivation. This is part of the awkwardness that is experienced. We are not accustomed to act, unless something motivates us to do so. The "what's in it for me" dies down pretty fast when one is in being. There is a natural inner satisfaction.

Still there is a need to continue to practice the presence and to go deeper within as part of integrating our everyday life into the new-found reality. This is why Gabor uses the phrase "Functional Silence". The wonderful silence is meant to be our dwelling place while maintaining our daily functionality. For this to occur, the deepening of presence through practice is essential.

So now I was finding that the pain of my dark night was assisting in this process. It was as if all those suppressed feelings were really my best friends. They were waiting inside me all this time so that when they became required as helpful catalysts, they were right there ready and willing.

Another important point to mention here is that when we free our pain, we free it up for others as well – our ancestors, children and anyone connected to us through similar pain and struggle.

6. Dear Women, Thrive on Your Gift

We are born ready!!!

A Woman has a tremendous gift. Her ability to withstand the horrendous pain of child birth; the dreadful anxiety and fear of losing a fetus that has become an integral part of her body; the intense love and protective care she has for her child; the total surrender and selflessness she adopts for her role as a mother; the painful letting go that is inevitable when the child becomes his or her own person – all these are no small feats. This makes her supremely equipped to take on the taskless task of turning within and awakening to the new dimensionless dimension.

She is not a stranger to pain. She is not a stranger to selfless love. She is not a stranger to radical transformation. She is not a stranger to rebirth. She is not a stranger to surrender. She is not a stranger to letting go. She is not a stranger to intuition. She is not a stranger to humility. She is not a stranger to losing what she has held so near and dear for so long. She is well equipped and has a built-in penchant for being elevated to a new world of love and magic. Even if she never has her own children, she would have picked all this up from the woman who gave birth to her.

So, beloved women, don't wish you were a man. Don't waste your time and energy competing with men. Don't squander your God-given gift by following masculine-like types of teachings. Once we accept this gift, it is easy as pie for us to turn within and rest in our own loving, comforting and nurturing feeling nature. This is our doorway to BEING HOME and all we need to do is use our gift to enter.

The feminine-like type of teaching that Gabor speaks of and

teaches is second nature to us and is very easy to access. We are ready. We have been prepared. We can easily teach this to others, as long as we are not lured by the mind that gets dazzled by the mind-based teachings. Feeling comes easy to us. Let us thrive on it!

7. Dear Men, You Have Free Access to This Gift

The ability to feel, to be humble, to surrender, to be willing to just BE without the need to conquer, control or do – is available to every man. Men have never been devoid of a feminine side. However, due to our faulty education (a man doesn't cry!), the manipulation of leaders who have been fanning the need to fight and protect for centuries, and the rapidly growing masculine types of teachings – there has been a marked imbalance of male-female not only on a global scale, but also on a personal level.

There are many techniques and practices that Gabor has developed to help foster and bring out the feminine-like nature of men and women alike. Gabor has many male students who have quickly and easily been able to break this pattern of spiritual male dominance and find their feminine-like ability to relax into presence.

Once the shift has taken place and one has entered the inner domain even for a short time, gender takes a back seat. To be able to use the gift of living and dealing with life's challenges from a new platform of BEING is everyone's birthright, regardless of gender. Divisions and differences have no bearing on presence. This is a new life and it matters not if you are a man or a woman.

8. Dear Men, Feminine Practices Will Not Make You Sissies

Some men resist having anything to do with a feminine-like teaching in fear that the feeling nature will turn them into sissies. Let me assure you that that will never happen. Gabor lives in his Queendom with great ease and dexterity and he is no sissy.

If you don't believe me, ask any samurai, if you can find one today. Attaining undistracted awareness of the present moment, and remaining in that state somewhat indefinitely, was a common goal of the samurai. The possibility of death at any moment was used as a fuel for cultivating this single-pointed awareness. This single moment awareness is presence. It is part and parcel of the feminine-like feeling of resting in one's body and being still. I am talking here about the samurai – the male warriors who conquered the fear of death... you couldn't have found a sissy or a wimp amongst them.

> There is surely nothing other than the single purpose of the present moment. A man's whole life is a succession of moment after moment. If one fully understands the present moment, there will be nothing else to do, and nothing left to pursue.
> – **Yamamoto Tsunetomo, Hagakure**

9. Ladies and Gentlemen! You Need Not Suffer!

Question by Ben Mango: *I find that when I am experiencing a tremendous amount of pain it is very difficult for me to go within. It appears that the pain completely takes over. What can I do?*

Gabor: *When we direct our attention into the body, we activate the body component which is basically the universe. Even though we have a huge pain in the body, whether it is physical or emotional pain, the heart is still beating, the lungs are still 'lunging', and the ears are still 'earing'. Everything is still working, right? So, by putting our attention this way [pointing within], we are activating the body's ability to handle this pain.*

We are not trying to shut down or change the pain in any way whatsoever, since this kind of pain also serves us as a catalyst. A catalyst is something that makes changes, but it itself does not change.

So, we have this huge emotional pain and we are trying to go into the body. In the beginning it seems almost like the emotional pain gets even more intense. Thus, people say, "Why should I focus on something that I want to get away from?" However, if we just stay with it for a little while, what we will find is that the body starts to activate, activate and activate and when it is fully 'activated', then all of a sudden, even though the emotional pain is still there, the suffering will stop.

It is very interesting to see that the huge pain is still there, but the mind is not participating by explaining to you why there is so much suffering. The mind stops coming at you with a narrative. The narrative stops, even though the pain is still there.

At that point it is a great catalyst, because you really have to focus on going within to maintain the 'no suffering'. Let's call

THE FEMININE PRINCIPLE: THE KEY TO AWAKENING FOR MEN AND WOMAN

this state 'no suffering while the pain is still there'. The next step I call the 'hug' [hugging himself]. The pain is still there, and with the activated body, I kind of surround and engulf the entire pain. Treat it like a welcomed guest (even though it is not so welcomed... ha ha).

So, I kind of hug it with this wonderful loving feeling of the transformational organ (the inner body). So, treat it like a sick child. Hug it and rock it as if it is a sick baby [Gabor puts his arms around his chest and makes rocking movements]. And do anything that comes to you at that point. For example, you can talk to yourself as someone would have talked to you when you were a kid. "It's ok little Ben, it's ok. Shh... it's ok."

The transformational organ now gets interwoven with the pain. We hug it, we love it, we treat it... we are not trying to change it, we are not trying to send it away and we are not trying to fight it. But what we are going to do is – for the first time we are going to let the pain have its own voice. It never had a voice. It was always treated like an unwelcomed guest: "Go away... I don't want to have anything to do with you!" Or we fight it with anti-pain medication and stuff like that.

So now we just hug it. The inner focus is still there, and we allow this pain to have a voice. Meaning, that practically, I open my mouth and whatever comes out, I let it come out with a hug [Gabor makes sounds like ooo... aaa]. You feel in your body which particular tone would be resonating with this pain.

So, you are treating it like a baby and making the sounds [Gabor embraces himself, rocks and makes the sounds – oooo... aaa. Shshshsh]. Experiment with it. Play with it. And all of a sudden you will find the tone. And it is the first time in its life that the pain has its own voice. This is what it was looking for.

This is what I would recommend. Unfortunately, many of my students have been practicing this. I am saying 'unfortunately', because some people have very heavy emotional pain. Eventually the intensity of the pain is lessened. The welcomed guest has had a voice, so the intensity is reduced, and the suffering stops almost immediately.

On the level that we are talking about that is the most that you can 'do'. This is an extremely important exercise not just for the pain, but also for transformation. Thus, the pain becomes your transformational buddy-buddy. You can still take anti-pain medication and do the same (as describe above). Both are ok.

Ben: *Thank you. This is very helpful.*

Gabor: *Very practical and I am telling you – it works very well!*

Nurit: *The concept of having pain without suffering is very foreign to most people, but it does work.*

Gabor: *Yes, it is a very interesting sensation. It is also a great experience to get to the point where the sensation is there, but the suffering isn't. So, what causes the suffering? Well, it's the mind's chatter. The mind is telling us that this is bad, especially with emotional stuff. It's mostly the mind's chatter that causes the suffering. It's a nice point to experience the difference between suffering and not suffering and amazing transformation happens at that moment.*

10. Ladies and Gentlemen! Claim Your Queendom!

What the world needs right now... URGENTLY! ... are not more spiritual smart statements and spiritual people competing over who can offer a better argument, explanation or dissertation on a gazillion-and-one impressive concepts. The world is saturated with and on the verge of suffocating from this masculine type of spirituality. It is filled with men and women who have been at it for decades with no meaningful results.

Global warming is not the problem... it's a symptom. Over-population is also not the issue. It is the consciousness or lack thereof of the population that is a huge threat right now. Too many people are fighting for their lives due to manipulative, greedy and unconscious leaders. But even the mean old dictators (including those who wear the disguise of democracy) are not the real problem. The overly popular and out of control mind is.

Too many pseudo awakened people are fighting in the name of ending the fighting, with a mind that has us believing that the battle will be won by being spiritual. There is no unity in that. There is no harmony in that. There is no balance in that. And there is certainly no peace on the horizon if this is allowed to persist.

The mind has conned us for so long that we have become totally oblivious to the fact that it has stolen our throne. It has held us captive for so many life-times, that many have lost their longing for freedom. They have given their power over to their oppressor, who has put them to sleep through its well-crafted mind-based spirituality. There are too many victims of 'spiritual Stockholm syndrome,' convinced that they can "think" their way into enlightenment. The slumber has become so deep, that we now have enlightened egos, dreaming that they are awake.

It may appear like spiritual progress, but we are so far removed from that. And yet, in a moment all can change. All that is required is a return to simplicity and a re-direction of our attention. We need to dethrone the mind and claim our birthright as rulers of our own Queendom. For now, it is being called Queendom, simply because it is the feminine-like nature that will restore the balance and bring us home. Remember, at this point gender is of no consequence.

We need to get out of our heads and into our bodies. Structured meditations and other masculine types of practices may offer relaxation, but this is still in the mind. A relaxed mind is still the mind. This is how it has conned us in the first place.

> *"A calm mind is not an indication that one is on the path to awakening. Neither is a busy mind."* **Gabor**

A new course is required now. By redirecting our attention away from the thought-stream and into the body through feeling, with no expectation, we activate the transformative nature of the body. We shift from relaxing in the mind to resting in the heart through the feminine-like feeling of pure being. This is your Queendom.

This is a tangible shift without which, there will be no true freedom from the mind. Once this shift happens, the mind starts to slow down or even becomes completely silent. This is the wonderfully satisfying feeling of being home and of "It's great to be alive!"

Going within and entering the body is so foreign to the mind, that it might tell us that it would be very difficult to do. This is not so at all. It is high time to stop believing the lies that our minds feed us and just go for it with radical abandonment of any mental strings that try to pull us back.

> *"Inner silence has nothing to do with outer silence."* **Gabor**

Chapter Four

Setting Free our Gift of Attention

A Guided Practice of Going Within & Re-proportioning the Attention

At the end of my interview on the Conscious.TV, Gabor was asked to guide us into inner body feeling. The video of this guidance is called "Gabor Harsanyi - Re-proportioning the Attention." Many people use this video for their practice and find it very helpful. Below is the transcription of it. (This video as well as the video of my entire interview, can be accessed through the Resources page at the front of this book.)

Gabor: *My attempt is to guide you to stay in the present moment. We usually call something like this meditation, but I don't like to call this meditation. I would rather call it the re-proportioning of attention. Normally our attention goes out and stays out. That is how we live our life. That's the expectation of others, of society, etc.*

By re-proportioning our attention, we keep some of our attention outside and some inside. If there is a consistent attention inside, and the attention is re-proportioned for inner and outer, then the mind will have a tendency to line up with the body. And when the mind and the body are in alignment, then you are in the present moment.

This present moment is not a small piece of time stolen away from time. It is out of duality. This is something that is your birthright. It is something that is very natural to every person and it's beyond time. Or I could also say it's in absolute time.

If you are just sitting comfortably somewhere, just keep looking at me and relax. Nothing major will happen. No expectation. And just for a moment feel the chair under your butt. Keep looking at me and feel the chair. [pause] Keep looking at me and feel your foot. What I mean by feeling your foot, is that you are aware that your foot is there. You don't have to look down to see if it's there. You're feeling your foot and you're feeling the vitality in it. You make it shine. [pause]

For those of you who are more comfortable in closing your eyes, please do so. Keep looking at me if your eyes are open and feel your hands. Be aware of your hands. Feel the vitality. Feel it shine. Feel the intensity, the aliveness in your hands. [pause]

And we will do the same thing with your chest now. Be aware of your chest. Focus on your chest. Make it shine. [pause]

Every breath you take will increase the intensity of this shine, will increase the aliveness of your body a hundred-fold. Every breath you take will increase the intensity. [pause]

Feel your shoulders. Be aware of them. Feel the vitality and make them shine. [pause]

Feel your thighs. Feel your knees. Feel the vitality and make them shine. [pause]

Feel your stomach. Make it shine. Every breath you take connects your so-called inner body and increases the intensity of this inner focus, the intensity of this inner aliveness. [pause]

If your eyes are closed, slowly open your eyes. But before opening your eyes, make a decision to keep some of the attention within. Of course, if you didn't close your eyes then you didn't close your eyes. We are keeping some of the attention within. [pause]

This is what we mean by 'The kingdom of God is within.' This is the simplicity of it. This is your birthright. This is the beginning of awakening, the beginning of spiritual learning. We are now beyond time, or I could say in absolute time.

Keep looking and feeling inside. There are no expectations. We are not expecting anything to happen. [pause]

One very important thing: this is not a meditation! Your mind would tend to tell you that this is the same as meditation. It's always now... it's always now... it's always now. Meditation is in time. It has a beginning and an end. This is the re-proportioning of your attention. I don't know what to call it. I will probably call it re-proportioning if I must call it something. The less I try to call it something, the better.

Just BE with me. [pause] This is the so-called knocking on the door that Jesus talked about. If your hearing has shifted a little bit, then the door is opening. This is the you that is already within you.

I didn't invent this. I didn't 'do' anything to you. I am simply sitting here looking at you. What's in me is in you and in every living thing. From this peaceful and nurturing perspective, it is not possible to have any harmful thoughts towards anyone or anything. Just keep being with me. No expectation. [pause]

Remember to keep some of your attention inside. Any body part will do. For most people the awareness of the hands from inside is the simplest. You might find that for you it's the foot or the chest. It doesn't really matter. One touch [touching his chest]... just one touch within is worth thousands and thousands and thousands of hours of doing something without.

It almost seems like you are willing to open the door to God by paying attention this way [pointing to the heart area of the body]. So now God, the universe, can be with you. Now your mind or my mind can operate form a different context. This is a contextual shift. You will not lose your memory. You will not lose your abilities. You are not going to become irresponsible. It's a perfectly functional space.

Stay here with me. [pause] What I am saying is not as important as your inner attention. You have to - if you want - focus within. No one can do it for you. It's easy. To look within, to try to go within, is very, very easy. Why should your birthright be hard? Why should your birthright take 20, 30, or 40 years to deserve by accumulating good deeds? It's yours now.

You can operate from this space. It's very functional. This is your being. This is how we were when we were children. It's not complex. It's not mind. By doing this you are not going to be a superior person, nor an inferior person. Life is going to be so much easier. Challenges will come, but you will know how to approach them.

Do this simple thing of re-proportioning as frequently as you can during the day while you are doing anything else. Standing in line at the store is a great way to practice. Washing dishes, washing your car, walking or talking. Try this as a listening skill. If someone has a tendency to talk too much, just focus within. Just BE and you will see magic happening in your relationships.

It's yours. You can only have it now. You can't have this in the future. It's now and now. Put this tape on as frequently as possible. Practice it and, most importantly, practice it in your everyday life. Don't allocate some time to practice it. Whenever you think of it, whenever it comes to you – now, now, now - re-proportion, re-proportion, re-proportion.

I wish for you to be able to maintain this natural state, although I cannot call it a state. With a little bit of attention and intention you will be able to maintain this. God bless you and all the love to you and yours.

Dear Mind, Butt Out if You Know What's Good for Me!

> *You've had your fun, dear mind. Now stop infringing on our birthright!*

The extreme ease and unfamiliar simplicity of directing the attention within and entering the body; the discomfort of losing control – these often send the mind into a tailspin. Hence, the mind tries to trick us into allowing it to reclaim its position as ruler and protector of our lives. Here are a few of the lies that the mind likes to feed us:

1. "This can't be a real experience... it is way too simple. There's got to be more to it than this." The mind has trained us for years to value anything that can become more and more, get bigger and bigger, be better and better. In the inner realm there is just "ISNESS" – nothing to add and nothing to reduce or get rid of.

2. "This is so boring!" The setting in of boredom is always a sign of the mind's involvement. It feeds on excitement and detests the seeming emptiness of silence. It is used to the flowery, exhilarating, and dramatic experiences of the masculine-types of teachings that require time and effort – the kind that provide a false sense of achievement and a spiritual self-image that we can take great pride in.

3. "This is just like meditation (or any other practice from the past)." It is only the mind that analyses, compares and categorizes. It is trying to pull us out of the inner realm and get us back to a relaxed state of mind, where it can remain involved. It keeps itself busy by comparing and then sweeps in as our savior by offering an altered 'state of

mind' through a well-established, approved by the spiritual society, meditation.

4. "Yesterday my practice of going within felt better." Again, the comparing process of the mind has kicked in along with its habit called 'expectation.' In the feminine mode of yielding into being there is no expectation. We knock on the door of our 'Queendom' by going into the body. The rest is up to the universe/God. As long as we are expecting anything, the mind has us by the balls.

5. "When will I ever find the time to practice this?!" It is only the mind that is in time – alternating between past memories, future fears, desires and expectations. The 'moment-to-moment'ness of being is not in time. It is not a separate event in time. It is not a thought. If it were, it would be impossible to engage it while being occupied in activities that require thinking. No two thoughts can be entertained at the same time. Since the 'moment-to-moment'ness of being is a feeling, we can easily keep a portion of our attention in this feeling mode while being involved in our day-to-day life functions.

6. "I don't feel anything. Nothing is happening." The mind is trying to interpret, qualify and quantify this new phase of inner being in the same manner that it does with all the other input and information it receives through the senses. However, it is not qualified to do so. Being, our inner Queendom, is beyond the reach of the mind and, therefore, no mind can judge what is or is not happening. Remember our caterpillar friends? They are not in any way qualified to evaluate the butterfly's affairs.

7. "I get it, but I wish it wasn't so." The mind starts to miss the mental activities and its involvement in the process. It wants to continue to strive and be acknowledged for helping us become enlightened.

> *"To look within is very, very, easy. Why should your birthright be hard? Why should your birthright take 20, 30, or 40 years to deserve by accumulating good deeds? It's yours now."* **Gabor**

Let's not allow our former captor to abduct our precious attention again. It might try to prevent us from making the necessary shift by getting us to 'think' about going within or perhaps even 'visualize' it. It does this just to throw us off our game and make sure we don't actually do it with our attention and feeling. The mind abhors being left behind. It will try to push its way back in and participate in any process it possibly can.

It will even go as far as learning everything we glean, everything we realize about awakening and the space of silence. It will then proceed to explain it back to us in duality terms and will run its own story about it. The mind in its current state is a thief that has no regard for anyone's copyright privileges. We must guard our Queendom with vigilant awareness. Once and for all let us establish ourselves in our new domain and take back the reigns.

And again, one of the mind's favorite strategies is to try talking us into doing traditional meditation. Meditation is in time. It has a beginning and an end. The mind lives in time and thrives on separation. It dreads and despises the unifying aspect of BEING PRESENT while doing our life. It wants us to carve out time in our day for the activity of meditation so that it would be segregated from all other activities.

Thus, by getting us to 'meditate,' the mind will lure us back into a time-based divisive practice in which we can go back to sleep in the world of mind-based spirituality, and BINGO! Guess who is covertly ruling us now!? I am repeating this point since Gabor and I have found this to be the most common excuse orchestrated by the mind. Most people don't like to hear this, but that is proof that it is so. It certainly has been my experience, and if I could spare anyone a few years or decades of never-ending time-base spiritual seeking, that would make me very happy.

> *For a big chunk of our lives the mind has been protecting us, guiding us, interpreting for us... for better or for worse – all the while holding the reins. We have been so entrained in trusting it, relying on it and, unfortunately, also identifying with it. We have become the mind to such a degree that we often mistake its messages for intuition or even for guidance from within. We think 'the Self' is warning us or advising us, when it is really just a mental regurgitation of old templates and narratives.*

Question: Sometimes, when I do the practices you gave me or when I am watching your videos, I get moments when I feel this peace. It feels like everything is ok and calm, but it is not an intense, a fancy or a dramatic feeling.

Gabor: From what you described, chances are that you have indeed experienced that peace. You mentioned it is nothing fancy. That's true. That's what it is. It is not fancy, and it is not intense. If a feeling is in the mind, it can be very intense. It can be an intense feeling of 'good'. The feeling in the body is not intense. The only reason that the mind-based feeling is intense is because it is always in relation to something else. It's intense because it swings - good to bad, happy to sad, etc. 'This' in comparison to 'that' is intense. When you go inside and feel this unifying feeling, it is not in comparison to any other feeling. So, the mind registers it as 'not intense'.

Question: The mind maybe feels not pleased.

Gabor: Yes, the mind feels not pleased. The mind says, "Why don't you experience my peace (the swing) so that I can participate with you." The mind wants to participate in the swing and feel good. It says, "Look how intense this is! Wooh! This is an exciting feeling. Excitingly intense!"

But this, the inner peace, is so calm. The mind is not participating. It actually is intense, but the mind can't compare it with anything and can't analyze it, so it says it is not intense.

"The only reason that the mind-based feeling is intense is because it is always in relation to something else. It's intense because it swings - good to bad, happy to sad, etc. 'This' in comparison to 'that' is intense. When you go inside and feel this unifying feeling, it is not in comparison to any other feeling. So, the mind registers it as 'not intense'." **Gabor**

The Frank Sinatra Syndrome - "I Will Do It My Way"

Every now and then we hear people say, "This teaching of presence and going within feels good, but I have to find my own way. Many paths lead there, and I have to find my own path."

This was good for Frank Sinatra and it is certainly true in spiritual duality. When one says this, it is a sure sign that he or she is listening to the feminine-like type of teaching (or any type of teaching, for that matter) through a mind. This is the habitual way of hearing and drawing conclusions in mind-based teachings.

In actuality, there is only one way of going within and every path that is mind-based leads away from it. There are many roads to duality teachings, but none to awakening. The direction is IN and the space is the silence of BEING. End of story.

I Am So Happy... I Must Be Present

For many years I sat in the presence of my former teachers feeling waves of bliss every time a glance or a smile was cast in my direction. The same joy would arise whenever a teacher uttered a smart statement that appealed to my mind or simply complemented me on my progress and understanding.

I was always surrounded by people who were in the same boat that was sailing through the shallow seas of mind-based teachings, enjoying the sun rays of intellectual understanding and exciting spiritual experiences that brought much happiness and a sense of achievement. I was being programmed to equate this kind of happiness with spiritual attainment, not realizing that ALL knowledge and ALL experiences are in mind. I know, this sounds horrible for the mind to read these words, but it has certainly been proven to be true for me.

One day, shortly after my shift in inner attention, I said to Gabor. "You know, I have been present for three days! This is so exciting."

Fortunately, Gabor doesn't miss a thing. So, much to my surprise and slight disappointment Gabor's response was, "Are you sure you were present?"

"Of course, I was present. I was so happy!" I responded.

"Being happy is not the same as being present." Answered Gabor. "You can be sad and be present. Presence is the stillness that accompanies whatever else you are feeling, as long as you give your attention to that inner silence. Presence, in and of itself, is not an experience, nor is it a mood or any kind of emotion – good or bad."

"But when I am present it feels good to me. So how can I know if I am really present or just happy?" I asked.

"You have to attempt to feel your body every now and again. You need to 'check in', so to speak, with your body. If you can go in easily, then you are present. Otherwise, it is just a happy feeling or a calm state of mind. You can still be happy, but make sure you are present as well."

Subtle point taken!

Chapter Five

Pursuing our Queendom is not for Wimps

Awakening is Not a Walk in the Park

When we do a google search, say for a hotel in Budapest, we immediately get hotel ads popping up on our screen - on Facebook or any other web page we open. Similarly, if we begin to have even a mild interest in awakening which, at first, we may think is the same as spirituality, we are suddenly inundated by numerous masculine types of new age groups and teachings, most of which promise us 'the best life ever'. We will enjoy everlasting bliss, ecstasy, exciting spiritual experiences, harmonious relationships, better careers, and most importantly – we will at last have total control over our lives and be able to manifest whatever our heart desires (which is really the mind's desire. The real heart is content!)

Most people (myself included) fall for this for various lengths of time, not realizing that neither themselves, nor anyone they know in their respective group has had any of the above promises fulfilled, let alone awakening. If you are lucky, or if you are the independent and rebellious type, you may be able to see through the bullshit early in the game.

However, if you are like I was – tenaciously holding on to false loyalty and the erroneous attitude of: "Never give up in spite of the glaring evidence that someone is screwing with my head" - you might linger on, only to have your so-called path dragged out to the point of spiritual exhaustion.

Either way, there comes a point when life throws us an opportunity by finding the right teacher or some shocking calamity, and we discover the feminine-like type of awakening. Then, there is no doubt in our heart of hearts that this is what we were really longing for underneath the glam and glitter of spiritual experiences and the promise of a perfect life.

Nonetheless, we quickly come to see that this new path that we finally arrive at is not a walk in the park. Going within is a piece a cake, but the integration part of this path is no picnic.

The feminine type of awakening is about release, surrender, letting go, submission to the 'moment-to-moment'ness of presence, acceptance of silence over our well-developed intellectual templates, the willingness to convert the way we think and feel and much more. The experience of peace is totally different as well. It is calm, subtle and not intense as are the feelings and sensations we have with mind-based spiritual experiences. On top of all that there is an eruption of many suppressed emotions and egoic tendencies that begin to rear their ugly heads.

WARNING!
This section may contain negative thinking.
Readers' discretion is advised.

I wrote a bit earlier about my dark night of the soul, and I am touching on this again here since it is such a 'make or break' point in the evolution of a freedom seeker. The most difficult part for me during the first few years was the anger and the shame I felt for having allowed myself to be spiritually fooled for so long. This was my self-blame phase. I hated myself and began to question my authenticity.

"I am such a fake." I used to say to Gabor. "If I were a sincere seeker all those years I would have found you or a teacher like you much earlier, instead of basking in my inflated and ever-escalating spiritual ego."

And Gabor would usually respond by saying, "At least you are now here. You know the answer and you know how to go within and BE HOME. So many of your former spiritual friends are still stuck in bliss. They are too comfortable to ever wake up."

At other times I would be furious with the universe or God. "Why didn't the universe wake me up earlier?" I would ask, as if the universe was some kind of gigantic malfunctioning alarm clock. "Why would I want to have anything to do with a God that let me be conned for so many years?!"

And then, when my mind was spinning out of control, desperately and vigorously trying to disqualify everything that threatened its supremacy, it would spew out any complaint it could about life on this planet:

"Life is a piece of shit. It is totally screwed up from the very start. Whoever was behind this creation must have been on 'crack.' I have never seen such poor planning!

"We are yanked out of the comfort and safety of our mother's womb into this hell hole of fear and insecurity that is all around us. We start off as colic babies with horrific gas pains and eventually graduate to excruciating teething agony, fevers, the flu and nerve racking diaper itches.

"While all this physical discomfort is going on, we start to pick up some unfamiliar vibrations of unconscious grown-ups - the dread of a panicking and controlling mother; a troubled father who is now tied down by family chains and financial stress; perhaps a jealous and vicious sibling; or overbearing grandparents who insist that everyone do things their way (the outdated way).

"Sure, there is also a lot of love, but it is nothing like the unconditional love that a baby arrives with. And very soon the original love, the initial wonder and our primordial innocence is dampened by mostly useless and stifling education. These are diminished by conflicting opinions held so tight by educated jack-asses who think they are so smart and advanced because they have more life experience and knowledge. Knowledge that they have received from equally deluded, unconscious and frequently insane people. And who can blame them? There is no manual on how to bring new beings into this world, and no one really gets what this world is all about.

"Congratulations to me. Now all the glory of my essential

nature that I came into this world with is gone. I am addicted to thinking, having goals, planning, being super busy, having deadlines, searching for answers, analyzing, judging, complaining (much like I am doing now), etc.

"I thought I got rid of all this by being spiritual. I tried so hard to transcend my 'humanness' and become enlightened. However, I failed miserably. Not only that, but I have developed really bad spiritual habits – I got hooked on visions and personal power; I became addicted to explaining everything intellectually and metaphysically; I got used to taking comfort in my mind's ability to understand deep spiritual concepts; I even took pride in 'thinking' that I 'get the value' of the emptiness of silence, so why bother actually BEING THAT.

"Now I must drop all of these old patterns and templates in spite of my reluctance to do so. I can't motivate myself to go within, since the motivation that I am accustomed to doesn't work here. I waited for so long to find and recognize my true being and now I have absolutely no doubt that this is it. And yet, I am resisting it and pushing it away. Why did I have to go through so many years of faulty programming just to get to the point of having to painfully strip it all off?"

Sorry for going on and on and painting a picture of doom and gloom. This is not exactly the material I would use for a motivational speech. I am sharing my experience here with the intention of exposing some of the thoughts that the mind regurgitates as it is gasping for its last dominating breaths.

In my case it was very much an agonizing push-pull internal conflict. If you have similar thoughts, don't worry! They go away as one continues the practice of re-proportioning the attention and going within. So, don't despair. I am here to tell you that it certainly gets better and easier. Best of all, the changes and improvements that occur are permanent. They don't die off like the highs that we get when we attend a two-week spiritual retreat.

Me: *There are so many growing pains and transformational distresses on the path of awakening, and not too many people want it. Most prefer to remain on the happy road of spirituality. So why should we bother to teach this?*

Gabor: *We have no choice. The universe is calling us all back home. Transformation is inevitable. Like it or not, we must wake up one way or another – either through pain or through practice.*

Oh! So that's What He Meant!

Awakening and learning to live from within our Queendom requires radical transformation. It can never be a 'continuation' of our previous spiritual pursuit. We have to be willing to relinquish long-term mental patterns and values and adopt new ones. It is essential to acquire a drastically different way of thinking. This is easier said than done, especially in the beginning of the process, when one cannot yet perceive how the mind works so hard to re-con us.

There are quite a few new concepts that are introduced in Gabor's book *Functional Silence* and in his lectures, Satsangs and seminars. These are foreign to the duality-based mind and they have not been ingrained into our mental syntax. Most of our lives we have been repeatedly receiving information that is contrary to our original being. Therefore, the new concepts that are designed to lead us home, must also be repeated over and over until one can grasp them intellectually at first.

When Gabor speaks he often repeats himself several times. This is not because he doesn't remember what he had already said. The reason for this is that he is not imparting 'information' in his lectures. He is rather acting as a bridge between the listeners who are still in the mind and the space of silence where he lives. The concepts and words expressed are frequencies that originate in the feminine-like feeling of being and uttering them repeatedly assists in breaking down the mind's resistance and pointing the listeners back to the stillness of 'no mind.' Thus, there comes a point when the participants no longer listen with a mind. They are now hearing the words and receiving them with their own conscious being.

As wonderful and as essential as it is to grasp these concepts intellectually, it is only upon experiencing them internally that one actually 'gets' them in a deep and meaningful way. Through repeatedly hearing them and by doing the practices that Gabor teaches, we suddenly get these moments of "Oh! So that's what he meant by..." We then realize that the intellectual understanding we had before, although necessary as a starting point, was superficial at best. Nothing can substitute the inner and experiential grasping of these truths.

And then, of course, there comes a point where even the new concepts are dropped. Gabor calls them 'cannibal concepts' since they consume old ones and, eventually, they devour themselves as well.

Hey Mind, Don't be a Schmuck... Please Cooperate!

For those who are stuck on the masculine-like type of teachings, where seriousness and acquiring hard facts are key components, this feminine type of awakening may not be for them. Once in our Queendom, our outlook on facts is quite different and being silly and weird are 'rewarded.' Surprisingly enough, for some this is not easy. When we came to this world we were care-free. As innocent children, facts mattered not, and weirdness was a foreign concept. Do we dare to return to that mode of being?

> *When we are spiritual, breaking the spiritual rules are 'thought' to be mistakes. In Awakening, breaking the spiritual rules is essential for freedom.*

Shortly after Gabor's book came out, he was interviewed by author and spiritual coach, Stefan Hiene. Here are some excerpts from this interview:

Stefan: *I looked through your book and came across your disclaimer. I have to read it. I love it.*

"Disclaimer: This is not a legal disclaimer. It is rather a 'facts disclaimer'. All the facts, used in this book, are believed to be correct. However, we cannot get to awakening by using 'proven' facts. Therefore, the explanations that are used in this book are based on how helpful or useful they are in reaching our goal. Once awakening has taken place, we can make up whatever facts we want."

I love this last sentence.

Gabor: *The whole point is that last sentence.*

Stefan: *Yes. I really like it. So, what is your approach. I noticed* *that there are some very technical parts in the book - some mathematical and geometric stuff in it. So, why this approach? Where does it come from?*

Gabor: *The reason I took this approach is because the attempt is to try to convince the mind: "At least temporarily, please cooperate. And here is some logic and reason. Please! Don't be a schmuck! Please cooperate and here is A, B, C and D. OK?"*

We need the mind's cooperation to some extent. Hence, we have some facts. Like I said, the facts are not proven facts. I can't prove them. But here is the difference. I was looking for facts that are conducive to awakening. Not necessarily factual. If we could get to awakening through facts, millions of people would be awakened by now with all the smart people around. There are some facts that I would say are conducive to awakening.

The easiest way to attempt to explain it in this short time is that the world we live in, the duality - or rather triality - world we live in is moving in a continuous horizontal plane. We are all searching on this duality plane for more and more and more and better and better and better. And many spiritually exhausted people hope that if they keep on going this way (horizontally), in time, they are going to get to awakening.

In other words, this 'now' is not ok, but maybe a year from now, that 'now' will be ok. We can go on forever like this doing the best meditations, the best teachings and everything, and it just keeps on going.

We've all heard the expression "Be in the now." And the reason for that is that awakening is in an angle to this reality (the horizonal line of time). If our reality is here [showing a horizontal like line], then awakening is in a 60-degree angle to it.

We can't 'continue' our way into awakening. We have to leap into it. I teach exercises on how to do that, and some of the exercises look very weird. So, if we are after being in the now, the now can only be reached now. The mind has to get used to,

"I can only reach my goal now, and what will take time is the integration." The goal (of awakening) is not going to come in time like everything else. It's going to come now, and integration will take some time.

"The NOW is not a small piece stolen out of time". **Gabor**

The exercises are inner focusing exercises using a whole bunch of faculties like laughing, inner feeling, etc. The basic exercise I have for entering the now I call the dolphin. It looks like a dolphin with a laughter like a dolphin. It's kind of weird [Gabor demonstrates]. These exercises are physiological and focused exercises.

Awakening has a kinesthetic derivative, meaning, that it is a type of feeling. It is not something that is visual. It is not hearing oriented, although the auditory sense is being used in the process of entering the body. So, physiologically we do all kinds of things to interrupt the mind. Instead of the mind interrupting me, I am going to interrupt it.

So, there are interruption exercises and once the interruption happens and the mind is cut off, the mind gives us a little bit of a break... like 20 seconds or 30 seconds perhaps. Then we enter the body and there is instant inner silence. Once these are practiced enough and repeated enough, we proceed to integrate our life into this silence, and there are different integration exercises.

Bottom line – instead of proceeding in the same way as we did before, which is not going to get us anywhere, the mind's own power is interrupted by my free will, and that interruption gives me a little bit of time to enter the body, to feel the body and to be in it. As soon as I am sitting in it, I am sitting on this new platform of reality.

It's a lot simpler than it sounds. The mind would label it 'hard' because it doesn't understand it. So, of course, the first thing we have to do is interrupt the mind that doesn't understand it. This is quite different... hence the book with explanations.

It is very much like pole vaulting. We leap into this new reality much like a pole vaulter. The pole vaulter runs, runs, runs, and the pole has to be put down in very solid ground for it to work. The information in my book is there to create this very solid ground so that, when we do the physiological exercise, we can leap with much ease, and the mind will interrupt much less.

Stefan: *I love this explanation. And I also like what you said that we have to realize that the goal is in the now. I think people don't realize that they can't chase a goal. It is not possible. You will not get there if you don't realize it's here. I am already content. I already feel like this goal is fulfilled, so I don't care if it comes in the future or not.*

$\mathcal{I}t's$ $\mathcal{N}ow$ or $\mathcal{N}ever$

> **Question:** *"How often should I practice turning within?*
> *All the time?"*
>
> **Gabor:** *"Not all the time… just NOW…*
> *and NOW… and NOW…"*

During my initial transformational difficult period, and especially when a lot of pent up and repressed emotions came up accompanied by insufferable resistance, I found it nearly impossible to practice being present. At times I wanted nothing to do with presence or going within. At the same time, knowing that this is what I had been waiting all my life to find, my mind would say, "Oh, shit! I am wasting so much time. After all those years of useless and unproductive searching, I can't afford to lose more time by not going into my new-found space of silence. How can I be so lazy and ungrateful?"

Don't you just love how the mind scolds itself? The mind never quits promoting its wonderful service of giving us feedback, even when it is not qualified to do so. It thinks it has jurisdiction over the awakening process. Can you imagine little red riding hood asking the wolf for its protection service?

Whenever the 'dark night' wave would finally subside by going within (often after having a conversation with Gabor), that wonderful feeling of being present would arise and fill my entire being. At those moments there was no doubt that I was in the NOW. Furthermore, there was no doubt that that NOW was always present. The sense of "I spent too much time away from the NOW" no longer existed, just as time ceased to exist. The realization soon dawned that it is only the mind that is in time and, therefore, thinks it has the right to offer its time-based commentary, which has nothing to do with awakening.

Buddha and the Fly

As part of our integration process, it is highly beneficial to practice going inside prior to performing any activity, so that we can be present while doing it, whether it is cleaning the house, speaking with someone or even creating a future plan. However, in my experience, this is not always easy to remember. We live in a fast-paced world and we are not used to this practice at all. Here again, we find that going against our habitual way of living is actually conducive to awakening.

But don't worry. You are not alone. Buddha had to practice this too. One fine day he was sitting quietly outdoors with a few of his disciples. A pesky fly kept hovering around him making its annoying buzzing sound. Buddha gently picked up a fly swat that happened to be there and with great compassion swatted the poor nuisance.

Almost immediately after putting the fly swat down, Buddha grabbed it again and gave the dead fly one more swat. "Why did you do that, Master?" Asked one of his puzzled disciples. "The fly was already dead after your first swat. It couldn't possibly become deader!"

"I was not intending to re-kill it." Replied Buddha calmly. "The first time I swatted the fly I wasn't present. It was a knee-jerk reaction to a disturbance. Hence, I repeated the action of swatting it making sure that this time I was present."

What worked for the Buddha can work for us as well. We can always repeat a thought, words or any activity while being present. This is an excellent practice. We need not worry about the time it takes for a repeat performance. It is never more important to save time than it is to BE.

As a type 'A' personality (whatever that means), being a triple fire sign astrologically, and spending years in the rat-race - both in spiritual organizations and in the corporate world with super important missions, high-priority projects and never-ending dead-lines - believe me, with all this in my arsenal, the last thing I would want to do is be inefficient or waste any time.

And so, every time I catch myself rushing through an activity to get to the next NOW, and whenever I notice how much energy I am leaking by overly prioritizing my day-to-day activities, I remind myself that "I don't have to be efficient. I just have to BE... present... NOW."

Then, having averted yet another mental tail-spin called - "What should I do first to make the best use of my time and be able to multi-task..."- I am back in that wonderful place of silence. From here it is very easy to repeat an action if necessary or to simply slow down and enjoy the 'moment-to-moment'ness of an activity without having a care in the world.

Obviously, if we just finished making dinner and realize that we have not been present the whole time, we need not throw dinner out and start over. This would be a good time to remember that being present is not in time. The moment, in which we become aware of this lapse, is a new moment, and it is a new NOW. Before the bloody mind starts to scold us, we can simply go within by feeling the body or following our breath.

> *"I don't have to be efficient.*
> *I just have to BE... NOW!"*

Chapter Six

Living Life from our Queendom

Life is Our Seminar

For so many years all my spiritual practices were applied as events that were separate from the rest of my life. Since I pursued mind-based spirituality, my activities were time-based and, therefore, segregated into time slots. There was time carved out of my days and weeks for meditation, chanting, study, attending lectures, Satsangs, seminars, retreats, etc. They were all 'scheduled' along-side my mundane existence and survival needs such as, making a living, taking care of my daughter, handling household affairs, etc.

My isolated spiritual routines were always held as priorities and my ongoing identity and self-image were of a spiritual person, as opposed to a worldly one. It is only in the realm of duality that we have separation, preferences and priorities. A spiritual priority is still a priority and, therefore, it elicits the 'desire-resistance' mode of living in duality.

Such was my life for so long – hankering over *'more'* spiritual time slots, and wishing I had 'less' mundane ones:

"Damn, if I could get by with 'less' sleep, I would have 'more' time for meditation and chanting."

"If only I had fewer ('less') household responsibilities, I could spend *'more'* time in retreats."

"I want to have 'less' worldly people to deal with. I need to be with spiritual folks so that I can have *'more'* metaphysical conversations."

"I hate life in the world. If only I had 'less' survival challenges. Life in the ashram was much (*more*) easier."

"Oye, another boring job. Why can't I work for my teacher? That would make me *'more'* spiritual, and much 'less' materialistic."

"I wish I didn't have to work at all. Then I could spend *'more'* of my time in spiritual activities, and 'less' time would be wasted on trivial pursuits."

"I don't like that person. She always talks about her kids and her problems. I want to talk '*more*' about God, and 'less' about the negativity of people's problems."

"I should spend 'less' time watching TV, and '*more*' time being engaged in spiritual pastimes that don't fill my head with extra garbage."

Notice how many times the words 'more' and 'less' came up in the above small-self-talk? This is a perfect example of how duality saturates spirituality – I want more, more, more of what I am programmed to think is 'good' and less, less, less of the so-called 'bad'.

This is how life is lived without the recognition of our unifying original nature. For years I have heard expressions and phrases such as, "Nothing is separate." Or "You have to live as though your spiritual life and mundane life are the same." Or "God is in all things and everywhere." Etc. But no one showed me how to do that. Most of the teachers who uttered those smart words were living in seclusion. They did not have to work in that god-awful and unholy thing called 'the world.' They did not need to struggle with relationships or have much to do with any everyday life challenges.

When the transformational shift happens, the time-based mind is no longer ruling us. There is a very different perspective on life's events and activities. In the 'moment-to-moment'ness mode of existence, as we re-proportion our attention and keep some of it within, we function in the so-called world from a unifying place of silence. We are holding God's hand, so to speak, while doing our life.

It is no longer a push-pull situation with time slots for wanted and rejected activities. The inner stillness, even if it is noticed by a small portion of our attention, becomes the background to the so-called outer events. It is felt as an 'accompanying' event to all other events. Our existence is recognized as the context that engulfs all our functions and activities, which are the content held in this contextual vessel.

In this 'uplifted' (for lack of better word) platform of living, everything is our seminar. We learn to integrate all of life's events, situations, circumstances, relationships, activities, jobs, duties, etc. with our re-claimed conscious awareness. Therefore, the excuse of not having time to practice becomes obsolete. Every moment offers us an opportunity to give some of our attention to our unifying beingness - thus, allowing it to accompany whatever is happening. Once this becomes our way of living, we begin to feel that there really is no inner or outer. There is only the nurturing underlying comfort of presence.

Question: I have been coming to your meetings and watching your videos and, at times of struggle, I still find it difficult to make 'being present' my priority, and to practice being present as much as possible. When my problems are screaming at me and taking all my attention, it is hard to convince myself to relax into the simplicity that you talk about. The subtle sense of being seems impractical to me. For example, I don't know how I am going to pay my bills this month, and that is all I can focus on right now. It is taking precedence, and nothing else can become my priority. Can you help me with this?

Gabor: So, the question is about being in the present moment vs. other things in life as a priority. This question in and of itself reflects a major problem in so-called spiritual teachings, which is that the inner silence or being present is considered to be content.

In other words, "I am going to study silence and do some meditation, then I am going to do some therapy, then I am going to do some past lives and crystals, and then I am going to take my kid to school. I am going to make some vegetarian food, and I am going to drive my car. Then I might do a little more inner silence."

I have just described the way inner silence is being used. Inner silence is being thought of as content. It's another 'thing' that I do in the context of my life. It's another thing that I do, preferably, after I have finished all my priorities. That is a huge misunderstanding.

Inner silence is a context. What is the difference between context and content? The easiest way to look at it is – if you have a bowl of cherries, the cherries are the content and the bowl is the context. Inner silence is not something that you 'do'. It is not something that you accomplish. Inner silence helps you become the real you, the real powerful you – the you that is holding God's hand.

At any moment of time I have a choice. Let's say I have a task. I want to drive my car. Do I want to drive my car as a limited being? or do I want to drive my car as a being holding God's hand... my superior self, my higher self? None of the words are good or adequate.

It's not something that we do occasionally. It is something that we need to be aware of every time we do something... actually, prior to doing something. This does not compare to other tasks. Let's say I want to make a phone call. I can just pick up the phone and talk unconsciously, not coming from the present moment. My mind can go on and on and on and on...

Or, alternatively, I can be aware of who I am. Coming from this context, the telephone call will be a hundred times more effective, a hundred times more loving and a hundred times more convincing.

When someone is asking a question as to what the priority is and considers being present, being in your body, as something that we 'do' - the question is already showing the basic problem. It is not the content. It is the context. Having the right context will totally amplify your abilities. It will increase your ability to be super powerful in your everyday life. It's what you are all *the time. So, don't use it as a priority. BE who you are and then address the rest of the stuff in life.*

To learn more about the topic of context and content mentioned above, I refer you to the chapter that begins on page 89 in Gabor's book "Functional Silence: De-mystifying Awakening for the Spiritually Exhausted". To access this book, see the Resource page in the front of this book.

Realization by Watching TV

On page 81 in his book "Functional Silence" Gabor talks about the radical and, to some quite shocking, practice that involves watching TV. This was a surprise to me too way back in the beginning of my tutelage with Gabor. My former teachers spoke against watching TV. For a mind-based path, this is not bad advice. However, when it comes to awakening the rules change. I would encourage you to read what Gabor says about this and how he prescribes using the TV as an advanced practice. Here's how I performed this technique and what has happened as a result.

Usually, not liking to watch commercials on TV, I was in the habit of muting the sound and/or trying to fill the time-gap with some practical activity such as, making some tea, starting with dinner preparations, sending a quick email, and so on.

Noticing how different my attention is when a commercial break takes place, I decided one day to take a new direction. During the silence of a commercial break, I took the opportunity to practice bringing my attention within by feeling my hands, feet, my butt on the sofa, etc. My mind became very quiet and there was the sweet feeling of loving presence. I did not want to let go of this wonderful feeling, yet the commercial was about to end and, of course, I wanted to continue watching my show. So, I set an intention to re-proportion my attention while watching the rest of the show and allow the inner silence to continue while another portion of my attention was back on the screen.

BEING... *in our Queendom is a 'feeling', not a thought.*

Thus, we can keep some attention on this inner feeling, even while being engaged in activities that require thinking.

It is a known fact that one cannot occupy two thoughts at the same time, which is a common excuse for not wanting to practice inner looking while being engaged in outer activities. This is true for all spiritual practices that are done on a mental level. However, while having my attention within on a feeling level and with a still mind, it became very clear to me that true presence is not in thought. Therefore, there are no two competing thoughts. I can "feel" BEING and have part of my attention on this feeling, while another portion of my attention is engaged in watching my show.

I did this several times and I even performed some of my usual practical 'during commercial' type of activities mentioned above, while keeping some of my attention inside. It felt like a warm cozy blanket of stillness in the background of events. I got that this inner attention, this peace, is the context, and everything else – the pictures on the screen, the melodrama of the show and the various activities done during commercials - these are all content.

I also noticed that when a particular episode on TV was sad or disturbing, it triggered my mind's association with what was transpiring due to stored up templates of past pain. When this occurred, I simply put more attention within, embracing the uncomfortable feeling that arose, and noticed that it melted into the loving background of my new-found context. Aha! So that's what he meant!

The Kitchen Chair Exercise

Question: *I noticed that when I am practicing being present, it stays with me until I have to do something. Eventually, I notice that the presence has stopped, and I need to remember to get back to it. Then I do something else, so again the present stops, and I have to remember again. So, do you have a tip that would help me to stop forgetting?*

Gabor: *This is extremely individual. What we can do is have a private conversation in which we can figure out what kind of a memory link in duality you have that could connect you and remind you. At the beginning, frequent reminders are wonderful. You can just sit and BE, and say, "What would it be that would remind me the easiest. What habit do I have daily that would remind me?" And then you can make a declaration to use it as a reminder and you will remember.*

I have been using this type of practice/reminder with tasks that I don't like to do. This way, not only have I gotten reminders, but eventually, as I have become present performing these activities, I have found that my resistance would fade away. This practice has done wonders for me.

I used to detest doing anything that had to do with the kitchen. I would cringe every time I had to even enter the kitchen. So, I decided to use this resistance as a reminder to be present. I placed a chair at the entrance of the kitchen. Every time I needed to enter the kitchen, my path was blocked by this chair. I did not allow myself to remove the chair until I was in my body and present. Then only I would go into the kitchen. This way I had a great reminder since I had to go into the kitchen several times a day. In addition, I eventually lost my intense dislike of being in the kitchen.

Now I no longer need the chair. However, I have in place several safety guards to prevent me from forgetting. The knob in my gas stove must always be held in for several minutes (perhaps it's only several seconds, but always seems longer) before the fire is sustained. So, whenever necessary, I use these moments for remembering or to simply deepen my presence by enhancing my inner peaceful mode of being, before any impatient waiting can creep in. Works every time!

Another example - the hot water tap in the kitchen does not shut off easily. I need to exert force to prevent it from producing a continuous annoying drip. Every time I exert this force, I use it to guide my attention deeper within.

These are just some examples that work for me. You need not do the same. You can simply get creative and find ways and situations in your life to use as reminders. Eventually you may not even need reminders any more. Presence will become your natural habitat.

The Magical Practice of Bypassing the Mind

Question: *What do you mean by bypassing the mind?*

Gabor: *If this is the mind that is coming at you [Gabor makes a hand motion by his head, suggesting waves of thoughts], bypassing means that we are not engaging the mind. We are not opposing it, we are not talking to it and we are not 'not talking to it'. We are really treating it like a friend who got lost, and now it is kind of talking, but we are not engaging it. We take our attention and turn it within very deliberately and with commitment. As long as we do that, and we don't engage the mind. We are totally bypassing the mind. This is the very basics of what I teach.*

Many people have now heard Gabor speak about the practice of bypassing the mind. He talks about this and demonstrates it at almost every Satsang, private session or seminar, and he has written much about this topic in his book "Functional Silence". Nevertheless, the question above keeps coming up by the same people who have heard his explanation several times.

This is not wrong or anyone's fault. It is simply because bypassing the mind is not something that we are used to doing. This too is a concept that has not been ingrained in our mental syntax. As a matter of fact, it goes against our habitual way of thinking. I was going to say that it is contrary to the way we use our mind, but we don't really use our mind. We were either not taught or we have forgotten how to use it. In any case, the mind is using us, and we have allowed this to go on for so long that we don't even notice that this is taking place.

The practice of bypassing the mind is of paramount importance for awakening and for protecting ourselves from the onslaught of the mind that wants to keep us dormant. It can be done either in a gentle way or in a forceful and deliberate fashion, depending on the situation, the severity of the mind's attack, or a person's inclination. Gabor usually advises people individually on this in private sessions and fine-tunes the intensity and manner of engaging this practice for each person.

This practice was not easy for me at first. My mind was so used to taking charge and trying to fix everything on its own, that it would even try to get involved in fixing itself. Now there's an oxymoron!

For example, I would get besieged by a powerful and relentless stream of thoughts that seemed impossible to overcome. My mind would jump in and try to rescue me by analyzing the situation, comparing these thoughts to others, figuring out how they originated, or what happened way back in my childhood that would cause them to be triggered now. Then it would start compartmentalizing them and commenting on the level of my advancement (usually giving it a very low grade), based on the category these thoughts were assigned by... yes, the mind itself! Get the irony here?!

> *We don't really use the mind. The mind is using us. We have allowed this to go on for so long that we don't even notice that this is happening.*
>
> *Bypassing the mind is the first step to re-claiming our freedom and taking back the reigns.*

Often Gabor would hear me say something erroneous, or even just look at my facial expression and he would say, "Stop right there. If you continue with this stream of thinking, you will end up in a tail-spin and create a whole new template that will never stop."

At first, I hated when he did that. As painful as some of those attacking thoughts were, they were mine and I wanted to hold on to them by figuring them out in my own habitual way. I was stunned to see how addicted I was to be used by the mind in this fashion (more like old-fashion).

I also became very aware that a mental tail-spin can seem so humongous and sticky, that the mind has us convinced that we need an equally gigantic solution for it. It cannot possibly fathom that the simplicity of feeling one's hand can do the trick. It will invalidate this simple act of feeling every time. Consider yourselves warned!

Eventually I caught on and realized the importance of bypassing the mind. I got that this is true surrender. There is no other kind. In all the mind-based teachings I used to pursue, there was always talk about surrender - one must completely surrender to God, surrender to the universe, surrender to a teacher or a teaching, etc. I could now clearly see that even the word surrender is not totally accurate. It is not that we surrender to someone or something greater. There is no such thing.

It appears we are giving up our addiction to being ruled by the mind, but even that is not really what we are 'doing'. We are simply disengaging the mind and its craft by turning within, and the mind naturally takes a back seat and loses its power over us. It is the mind that is forced to surrender. However, as long as we identify with the mind we say we are in the act of surrender. In the next section is an example of how I practice bypassing.

Shifting Attention – Building the Muscle of Awareness

Gabor and I often go to our favorite coffee where we do most of our writing. One morning I was particularly motivated and eager to get there fast in order to spend as much time as possible doing our 'work.' So, you can imagine my frustration upon discovering that I forgot to bring my wallet with me. This was the wallet that had our spending money in it. It seemed like the only solution was to go back home and get the wallet, while Gabor waited for me at the coffee shop.

My mind started its habitual activity of weighing the pros and cons of having to perform this unchosen and undesirable task – "Damn, I am losing precious time. Maybe I don't need to have money on me." "Maybe something good will come out of this." "Maybe I will bump into someone nice on my way." Etc.

I very soon realized that there is no way around this, and that my mind was trying to take over by fanning the flames of worry and agitation. I decided that this would be a good time to practice bypassing. Even though I was on my way home alone, I could practically hear Gabor uttering his 'stop right there' message.

Rather than getting pissed off at my mind for its sneaky attempt to infiltrate the situation and hijack my attention, I simply began to feel the wind on my face, notice my breath and feel my feet on the ground as I walked. Within seconds my attention was averted and released from the grip of the mental activity surrounding my unwanted circumstance, and the inner feeling filled my being.

As I was sitting on the subway, I observed a nice family with two little boys sitting across from me. My attention, once again, was hijacked by my mind, who was now enjoying watching (or rather interpreting what my eyes were seeing) this family and making its usual commentary – "They seem so happy. The boys are cute even though they are cross-eyed. The husband and wife look like they still love each other. The husband must be focusing on making money to support this family. The wife is totally absorbed in these kids..." and on and on... And I noticed that, once again, my mind and its duality-based templates seduced my attention to go after its 'meaningful' (not!) observations.

Once again – feeling my breath... feeling my butt on the seat... being in my body - to the point of regaining my attention by disconnecting from the tentacles of the mind and redirecting it within. Now I am still noticing this family, only this is happening from within and with a still mind. I am seeing them with love, not with labels.

I used to be so upset with myself when I couldn't keep my attention within for a long duration of time (as if it were in time). That day on the subway, I finally realized why Gabor kept telling me that - more important than staying present for a long time is how often I catch myself and bring my attention back within. It became so clear to me that - the repeated practice of leaping out of the mind's hold, and freeing my attention to go inside, provided me with a great opportunity to build the muscle that would propel me and steer me in the direction of my own Queendom.

Noticing vs. Observing

During that subway ride home to get my missing wallet, I also realized the vast (although rather subtle) difference between observing and noticing. In observation there is always some sort of mental adjudication and the mind is justifiably free to make commentaries and spin stories about what is being observed... including the good feeling that accompanies the "now I get the 'observer and the observed' spiritual concept."

In noticing there is no engagement with the mind whatsoever. This, of course, can only take place when the mind is bypassed, and the attention is welcomed back home. Unless the mind is stilled by going within and activating the inner body, the noticing that I am talking about here will not be authentic.

We perceive with one or more of our senses (mostly through the eyes or the ears). In noticing there is a knowing/recognition of what is being perceived, but that's where it stops. There is no mind interpretation accompanied by the biased opinions that are stored in our mental templates. With noticing a person or a thing is seen as is.

In observation, on the other hand, whatever we see may be described, compared, analyzed, categorized and stored as a memory that either re-enforces an existing template or creates a new one. The object perceived is no longer just a vase with flowers, a human being or a spiritual experience. There is the accompanying commentary that goes something like this:

"Oh, that's the vase I got from my grandmother before she died. She really liked it, but I don't care for it much. Maybe I will get rid of it."

"That man looks so familiar. Where have I seen him before? I wonder if he is the pervert they showed on the news? Nah, he just looks like George Clooney."

"This vision I am having right now in my meditation is not as powerful as the one I had yesterday. I am observing it, so I must be the observer, but who is observing the observer? I wonder how much time is left before I can get up and tell my teacher and friends that I had this observation. I wish meditation wasn't so boring."

Thus, the danger in observation is that by allowing the mind's interpretation, we are permitting it once again to seize our attention and drag it though yet another endless 'thought-stream' that fortifies the mind's important position as CEO of our information center. Having the awareness to catch this before it goes too far, switching to noticing by bypassing the mind, and keeping some of the attention within - these are the greatest gifts we can give ourselves.

Hence, my uncomfortable situation of having to go home and get my wallet turned out to be a great seminar. It was a most valuable opportunity to practice and realize the efficacy of noticing, redirecting the attention and leaping out of the mind on a very deep and intimate level.

By engaging life this way, it becomes very clear that all the events, activities, observations and explanations that go on are the content of life, while the background of inner attention in a feeling mode is the context in which it all occurs. This brings us back to the point of being committed to living as the steady and silent context while noticing the ever-changing content with its ups and downs.

> *In noticing there is a recognition of what is being perceived, but that's where it stops. There is no mind interpretation as in observation. This can only take place through bypassing the mind, going within and activating the inner body.*

The Princess and the ~~*Pea*~~ *Be*

I am sure you've all heard of the famous story written by Hans Christian Andersen, called the *Princess and the Pea*. Just in case you haven't – it is about a princess who was very sensitive and no matter how many mattresses were piled underneath her, if there was a single pea under them, she could feel it.

Gabor and I are much like that princess. I doubt that we would be able to feel that poor suffocating little pea, however, we are very particular about the mattress we sleep on. And, no, this has nothing whatsoever to do with being in our Queendom. This is just a build up for my next story.

Not too long ago we had a fire in our apartment and just about everything burned down (more on that catastrophe later). After days of sorting through the black mess, followed by a very stressful and exhausting move, we realized that we had no mattress. Oops! I guess making a list of everything that is lost is not the same as making a daily or weekly shopping list. Our special Swedish memory mattress was destroyed in the fire. It was already quite late, and I was falling off my feet with fatigue. But, sleeping on a rough old couch was not going to cut it.

So, dragging my aching body, off I went with Gabor to a store that carried the kind of mattress that we wanted. This store was in the biggest mall in Budapest. In my extreme exhaustion, this mall seemed so enormously huge. "The *New Jersey State Garden Mall* looks like a fancy kiosk compare to this place." I mentally mumbled to myself.

We walked and walked and walked and finally got to the right store. By now, I was no longer just exhausted... I was ready to faint any moment. So, you can imagine the panic button that was pressed in my head, when the clerk said that they no longer sold that particular mattress at the mall branch. OYE! This was my one-time brief 'back-in-mind breaking-point' during the fire episode.

Seeing my disappointment and desolation (an understatement of all understatements!), the nice lady at the store proceeded to explain to Gabor how to get to their other branch. This was 30-40 minutes away and required us to take a bus, a subway and a little (nothing was little by now) walk.

"There is no way." I whispered to Gabor, barely able to get those feeble words out. "I am blacking out. Please, let's just go home. I don't even know if I could make it home." Gabor took one look at me and instantly agreed. "Of course, we can go home. We can take a taxi if need be."

As I leaned on him with desperate attempts to crawl out of that mall, taking very slow and frail steps and barely able to breathe, Gabor gently reminded me of the practice of going into my Queendom. "Sometimes it is actually easier to do this when you are exhausted." He said. "Your mind is too tired to put up a fight. Go back in if you can."

As I continued this seemingly long, arduous and grueling tread, struggling to get to a nearby cab, I began to pay attention to my breath – inhaling and exhaling slowly with increasing awareness and steady rhythm. As heavy as my legs felt, I was still able to feel my feet on the ground, so I sent some of my attention to that feeling.

Now, you may not believe this, but I kid you not! Within less than a New York minute (sorry New Jersey) – I was so totally recharged, that I stood up straight, released Gabor's supporting arm and said, "Let's go and get that mattress. Your teaching is amazing. It works. I am fine."

Long story short... we got the exact mattress we wanted with a very good discount and had the best sleep ever that night... no pea... just BE!

It Just Ain't the Same No More...

Most people don't like change. We seem to have so much fear of the unknown. This fear is not ours. It is an implant that somehow was installed in us. Our computer-being has been hacked and the virus of fear was installed on our hard drive. We came into this world with no fear. I still remember how my daughter used to leap out of her father's arms like a frog when she was a baby, never fearing that she would fall and get hurt. There was no doubt that daddy would catch her.

It is only later in life that our mind adopts the emotion of fear as a means to warn and protect us. The problem is that the mind is not very intelligent... certainly not as intelligent as the universal consciousness is. When the inner shift takes place, a lot of this fear comes to the surface to give itself up. It was a huge and rather embarrassing revelation for me to notice how little trust I had in the universe... how fear of the unknown had crippled my flow to the point of trying to control everything in life.

During all those years of spirituality I was sure this was conquered. "Of course, I trust the universe! I am a spiritual person! I trust my Guru. I trust life since that is how I am supposed to appear as a spiritual person who thinks positively." And then I woke up and my true colors – a vulnerable human being inundated with fearful templates – showed up.

The more I practiced living in the moment, the more I realized how ridiculous it is to fear the future. First of all, the future ain't here yet. And secondly, we have no proof it ever will be! My mind wrestled with this for a while in my early days of discovering my Queendom.

And then, one hot summer day in Toronto, as I was driving out of a very crowded parking lot of a shopping center, something so simple, yet highly illuminating (it's not always the big stuff...) happened. To paint you a better picture I must first tell you how much I detested driving. Driving was never fun for me. It was always accompanied by anxiety and stress, especially when making a left turn. Years ago, before I could even drive, I was a passenger in a terrible car accident that occurred in the midst of a left turn... 'nuff said.

So, this day, after doing my usual big weekly grocery shopping, I got into my car and started heading towards the exit of this huge shopping center. The exist was quite far, but from a distance I could see that not only did I need to make a left turn to get out, the rush-hour traffic was horrendous.

"Holy shit!" I mumbled to myself. "I will never get out of here... alive!" I quickly scoured the area in search of other ways to drive out, even if it meant taking a longer route to get home. But alas! No way but to face my enemy – the dreaded rush-hour left turn.

It suddenly dawned on me (kind of out of nowhere) that I was worried about a future event. A very near future event, but a future event nonetheless. "At this moment I am not there." I said to myself. "I am not there yet. I am not at that dreaded place yet. I am still in the parking lot, not at that busy street. Right now, I am here. Right now, I am safe in my car."

With this declaration I proceeded towards the exit. And wouldn't you know it! No... there was no accident and I didn't die. I am here alive telling you all about this experience, aren't I? At the very moment that I reached the spot where I had to get onto the road, there was a big gap in the stream of oncoming cars. It was as if dear old Moses parted the traffic just for me and allowed me to make my left turn with ease and serenity.

If this wasn't a great confirmation, I don't know what is! "In this moment all is well." I stated to myself. "All my anxiety came from being 'not here... not at this moment.'" From that day on, whenever a future event is accompanied with fear, worry or panic, I simply say to myself (or to my mind, rather), "I am not there yet."

> *Two minutes before writing the story I just wrote,*
> *I had no idea that it would be shared in this book.*
> *I was not there yet.*

Chapter Seven

Law of Attraction is not what we 'Think'

The Missing Ingredient in the Manifestation Process

Question: *I have been into Law of Attraction for many years, with little to no success. I watched The Secret several times and I followed the practices recommended such as – defining my goals, making a list of what I wanted to manifest, making a vision board, etc. I also attended many Law of Attraction seminars.*

I really want to manifest a better paying job, but all my efforts seem to go nowhere. I have met a lot of people who are in the same boat. I am beginning to think that Law of Attraction works only for a select few. What am I doing wrong? How would you recommend that I go about manifesting my dreams?

Gabor: *This is a wonderful question that people ask frequently. We, of course, consistently want to make our life better and rightfully so. This involves our manifestation process. This process has two main components: a. Defining our goals and what we want to create and b. Letting go.*

The first component is usually done with the mind. This is the more popular one. It is the masculine-like type of co-creating that most mind-based Law of Attraction lectures and seminars focus on.

You must have heard of defining and re-defining your goals – hear it, feel it, touch it... as if you already had what you wanted to manifest. So, if you wanted to manifest a red Ferrari, you would see its bright and shiny color, you would smell the leather seats, you would feel what it would be like to be in it and drive it - its great acceleration, the rush you feel when you take a turn, the tremendously exciting speed... and, of course, you might also hear the sirens coming behind you to give you a speeding ticket. That's just beside the point!

If you wanted to manifest a partner, you would define the looks, the smell, the touch of the partner. You might feel that you are holding hands walking along the beach.

So those are the popular mind-based ways to define what you want, how to work with your mind, how to reach your goals and how to manifest things. It is an extremely important part. However, because you do it with your mind, you are automatically creating major obstacles.

When we attempt to define our goals with the mind we fail to realize that our choices and desires are tainted by our conditioning. They are influenced by the mental templates that we have developed and stored away.

Also, the mind is in duality. Most 'wants' spring from 'lacks.' We want to manifest more money, because we have a template of lack created by difficult financial life situations. Even if you do succeed in manifesting a mind-based desire, you can be sure that the opposite from which it originated is not far behind. When the pendulum swings back it can hit you like a ton of bricks.

In spite of the fact that there is so much controversy surrounding the topic of Law of Attraction, it seems to be one of the most sought-after pursuits among new age seekers today.

There are so many law of attraction books and videos attempting to fulfill the ever-increasing demand of those who are seeking a better life.

Guess what's behind this demand for a better life – fear, lack, separation... the very ingredients that prevent us from manifesting a better life!

When it comes to Law of Attraction, it is much better to adopt the feminine-like type of approach of feeling and surrender to being. It would be far more productive to clear yourself of all thoughts, by relaxing into the empty space of presence and allowing the Universe to bring you what is essential for you.

You may make suggestions to the Universe, but if you are still and resting in silence as you do so, you are merely whispering to the universe instead of screaming at it. The more you want something, the more you are telling the universe that you are dissatisfied with what you already have. This is resistance rather than a state of acceptance, where the universe can just pour its gifts unto you.

We live in a fear-and-greed-based society. Greed is just another form of fear - "I must have this, so that I can protect myself from not having it." If we are not creating from an awakened place that is beyond these emotions, we will simply continue to perpetuate and manifest more of the same.

The other danger of defining your goals with your mind, is that the mind now becomes like a mother who doesn't want to let go of the child she gave birth to. This brings us to the second component of the manifestation process – the 'letting go' part. This is just as important as the first, however, it is impossible to achieve it, as long as the mind is involved. This is the secret that they keep from you... even those who talk about 'The Secret'.

We are told that once we define something, we must let go of it before it can manifest. And yet, most people don't have success with this part of the process. And we wonder why we can't manifest our dreams! Again, because the mother that gave birth to a child – a mind that gave birth to a goal - does not want to let go.

At best the mind will try to regurgitate what it heard in a seminar, "Ok, speak in present tense. Don't speak in future tense." That's not good enough.

*Or the mind will say, "Ok, I will just let it go." But there is a huge difference between the 'thought' of letting go vs. actually letting go. The inability to let go is the biggest obstacle in manifesting our dreams. The mind will simply **not** let go.*

Question: *So how do you let go?*

Gabor: *Well, if you do the first component of the manifestation process without the mind's interference, it will automatically be taken care of. If, however, your mind has somehow managed to take over again and tries to take credit for this process, it's ok. It happens. You can let something go by feeling it in your body. I am trying to give you a very short course on a much longer process.*

Your mind works with your senses - your hearing, your sight, your touch, etc. - those are limited senses. The letting go process involves a much bigger sense - an unlimited organ or sense that you have. That's your own body. This has totally been neglected. It has not been talked about, nor has it been researched.

You let go by using this biggest sensory organ and you learn how to pay attention to the 'inside' of your body. You do it with the body. By doing this, the mind that normally goes back and forth, back and forth, back and forth will finally slow down. The mind that thinks it can successfully define your goals will now give up and become still.

So, you have to learn how to pay attention within the body. The result of that is that the mind will halt. You will be able to define your goals without the contamination of your mental templates. You will have the skill to prevent the mind from holding on to its creation. I suspect that this is what you have been missing. I wish you all the success with your manifestations.

"To attract something would imply that it is separate — 'I am here, and I want to attract something that is there.'

To create something, we need to BE with it... be unified with it. In Hungarian the word 'attraction' is 'vonzas', which also means BEING. It is the act of BEING." **Gabor**

Procrastination is Not Lack

Another way that the masculine type of spirituality has infiltrated the process of manifestation is through duality-based smart sayings and pseudo motivational concepts. Most of these are time-centric and action-oriented. They are not 'BEING NOW'-oriented and, therefore they are misleading. They contribute greatly to our fearful and dormant state. Of course, there are some good and more accurate inspirational expressions as well, however, upon awakening, even those are no longer relevant.

For example, "Don't do tomorrow what you can do today", or "If you want something, go get it! Make it happen!" These are some (to name a few) that I heard pretty much throughout my life and tried to abide by. The same concepts were echoed in different words by some of my former spiritual teachers.

One of them used to utter statements such as, "Procrastination is lack" and "Procrastination is the onset of the deterioration of the will". The latter may be helpful for seekers following a masculine type of teaching, where one's personal will is what keeps one going, and where there the much-needed spiritual will is discussed at great length.

In the feminine-like type of teaching this is neither useful nor accurate. Being and living in our Queendom does not require a strong will. Here the deterioration of the personal will is what is needed as one surrenders and relaxes into the body, which is run by the universal will. This is where BEING is the key to everything and the 'doing' is secondary.

It may appear as procrastination to a mind that cannot fathom non-dimensional feeling, but it is far from being any kind of delay tactic or a resistance to act. The will here is the willingness to just BE, and the act is one of pausing in silence and allowing the creative power of the universe to dictate the next move in a timeless fashion.

> *Allowing ourselves to just BE... before jumping into action is not procrastination... no matter how long it takes.*

Spending all those years in the masculine type of teachings intensified my will and caused me to be extremely action oriented and impatient. I would not be caught dead as a procrastinator. I was always early for every appointment and met dead-lines hours or days before they were due.

This came in handy in the corporate world and awarded me great reviews. However, it became quite a hindrance upon awakening. It was especially a real nuisance while working with Gabor. Frequently, in our meetings and conversations, as soon as an idea was presented by either Gabor or myself, I would become anxious to get up and start implementing it. Many times, Gabor had to stop me by saying, "This is an 'idea' meeting, not an 'implementation' session. Just BE with it."

Thus, I learned to use presence in the midst of planning, strategizing and setting goals. In this context the 'pause', which others may call procrastination, has also been proven to be extremely helpful when faced with dilemmas or situations that do not lend themselves to quick and easy solutions. Through the practice of going within and being present I learned to just BE with a situation, a question or a problem instead of rushing to resolution. Whenever this is done, I am always amazed at the miracles that take place.

This is precisely how this book is being written – I never plan or know what the next paragraph or chapter will be. I sit and be... and the words begin to take off and form what you see on these pages. This is done with the help of a mind-skill that I can summon to assist when needed. The pauses of 'being' that I take do not in any way prolong the writing process. On the contrary. When the writing is happening, it moves so rapidly, that my hands and brain can hardly keep up.

> *Many wild animals remain very still and quiet before leaping upon their prey, no matter how hungry they are. They are present. They pause before rushing to the attack. Do they know a great secret, or have they simply been spared the 'don't procrastinate' indoctrination?*

The other day we had to find a textile store in our area in Budapest since we needed to purchase a very specific type and color of material for the background of our videos. We did the usual google search but came up with no results. We opted to let the 'doing' and the 'effort' go and 'just be with it.'

As we began to head out for lunch, we decided to try out a new restaurant. So, we walked on a street that we usually don't take. After two blocks, there to my right was a beautiful textile specialty store. We walked in and right in front of us was a role of the exact type of material and in the exact color that we wanted.

These kinds of things happen to us all the time. We may not be highly motivated, ambitious, driven, fast-paced go-getters like we used to be, but relying on the universal CEO certainly beats being at the mercy of a managing mind with its turbulent and restless willfulness.

Let's Not Confuse 'Waiting' with the 'Pause' of Being

The more modern new-age Law of Attraction instructors have managed to bypass the procrastination risk by telling us that "Good things come to those who wait." They encourage us to be patient and wait for the manifestation goodies to come to us. It certainly seems like a step in a better direction, but waiting and BEING are light years away. In waiting there is expectation, which is very much encouraged in Law of Attraction popular methods. However, expectation is in the mind – "I really hope I can manifest this promotion. But... I can wait. Nonetheless, I expect it to be mine. I worked so hard and I deserve it. I even put it on my vision board, which I look at every day. Why is it taking so long? Oh, yeah, I have to be patient." – and on and on it goes... Without the stillness of presence, the mind just ain't letting us off so easy.

In BEING there is no waiting and no expectation. There is no need to practice patience, since there is no mental interference that needs to be tamed. There is simply BEING. There is silence and allowing. There is the holding of God's hand or being in the flow with the universe – whatever you wish to call it. We are not chasing something or pretending to wait for something in the name of spiritual creators.

When I was pursuing the Abraham Hicks Law of Attraction teachings and practices, one of the most frequently asked question that came up in the seminars was, "Why is there such a long gap between the time that we define what we want and the time that we actually get the 'goodies' we've asked for?" Usually this was asked by people whose 'goodies' never came at all, but they were still waiting with hope and expectation.

And Abraham would explain that this is due to the fact that we live in time. Well, guess what else lives in time? Yes, the mind! When we attempt to manifest through the mind, we are in time, and there is no telling when 'the time will come... if at all' for our desires to manifest.

When we are in BEING, on the other hand, when the mind is subdued, we are no longer in time. Thus, it would be quite natural for our co-creation to manifest instantaneously. Of course, we would call it a miracle... but is it? Or is it simply the most natural thing to occur, when the Universal intelligence is taking the lead?

Manifesting the 'Right Partner'

> Manifesting the 'right partner' is not the same as manifesting a conscious partner. But, of course, to manifest a conscious partner one has to be at the very least semi-conscious.

For many years I dreaded being in a relationship. It took me 18 years of being alone to finally make a change in this aspect of my life. The very thought of marriage or any form of a committed relationship gave me waves of depression. All I could feel is the pain of two minds or rather two egos clashing against each other trying to win an imaginary power struggle. And this is exactly what happens when a couple is unconscious.

Shortly after my parents were divorced, my father found a most compatible girlfriend. He was a sculptor and she was a painter. They were both wonderful artists and very much in love. They had so much in common and best of all, they shared the most valuable interest and penchant - art. It seemed like a match made in heaven. The only thing they each lacked was the awakened consciousness.

One day, as they were both enjoying doing their respective art work side by side in my father's studio, my father got very hungry. He was covered in plaster and other compounds he was using and so, he asked his beloved girlfriend if she could please make him a sandwich.

Her reaction was most unexpected. "How dare you ask me that!" she said in a raised and scolding tone. "I am also an artist and I am doing my work just as you are. Make your own damn sandwich! If you think you can treat me like your servant, then I can't be with you anymore." She then packed up and left.

My poor father was stunned. He had no idea what hit him. He was going to marry her. He had already picked a ring, and with one thought she put an end to his entire dream of sharing his life with another artist who, supposedly, understood him.

Forty-five years later, many years after my father had passed, this old girlfriend happened to be in Toronto, where I was living at the time. She looked me up and requested to see me. I was surprised. She hardly knew me. I was a teenager when I met her briefly and later I learned that she didn't even remember meeting me at all. So why did she want to see me?

Anyhow, I met with her where she stayed in Toronto and that's when I heard for the first time, that they broke up over a sandwich. But wait... there's more...

She never got over my father and never had anyone in her life again. She was heartbroken when she heard that my father re-married a few years after she left. So, here she was with me now at a very old age confessing about how much she still loves my dad and yet, she can't possibly forgive him for requesting a sandwich. Really???? I didn't know if I should laugh or cry. Oh... the madness of the unconscious mind! It can so easily destroy such a beautiful love.

Thus, my father, in his unconscious state manifested a partner who seemed to have the potential of being the 'right partner' for him, but not a conscious partner.

> *How much do we really have 'in common' with another if the madness of the mind is running our lives?*
>
> *There is no worthier common ground than consciousness – our unifying presence.*

This is precisely why it is imperative to awaken and allow consciousness to come into our lives and affairs, if we ever hope to be in a relationship that is based on peace, silence and unconditional love.

Manifesting My Conscious Partner in My Semi-Conscious State

When I finally decided that I was ready to throw myself into the ring of 'being in a relationship', I went to all the Law of Attraction seminars, read all the books on this topic and spoke with any smart manifestation expert within shooting distance and beyond. I made my list of all the things I was looking for in a partner. I didn't know what a conscious partner was. My list only consisted of qualities that I wanted in a man that I could call my 'perfect partner.'

I wasn't awake. I was in my mind and that is how I was pursuing this goal. I went to all kinds of singles' meetings and joined several online dating services. I even went on many dates, but no one felt right... including the supposedly spiritual men and those who matched most of the characteristics on my extensive and well calculated list.

Nothing worked. My Law of Attraction efforts failed miserably. I was receiving the Abraham Hicks CD's every month, listening to them over and over again and practicing what I heard – nada! I was not one of the selected few successful creators. I was not one of the lucky happiness seekers who fell through the cracks and somehow managed to get good results.

This went on for five years before I was able to manifest Gabor as my partner, not even knowing that he was conscious. It happened shortly after a lunch that I shared with a dear friend. During our conversation, I mentioned to her how I was struggling with this manifestation, even though I created such a good list. Her only comment to me was "Throw out your list! Get rid of it."

As shocked as I was (and somewhat perturbed) her words rang

true. I now know that making a list is really an attempt to carve expectations in stone. But back then I didn't realize this, so it was with a heavy heart that I threw out my beloved list. Within a few weeks, the most important event in my life took place – the event of calling Gabor and deciding not to think while with him, which I wrote about earlier in this book. (More on that is narrated in my first book, *The Blind Leading the Blonde*. See Resource page to access it.)

That was my first step in being semi-conscious, and it was the only way I was able to recognize the conscious being who would become my partner. The amazing things was that Gabor, apart from being a handsome man, matched none of the qualities that were assembled on my list.

He wasn't rich, and he wasn't hilariously funny. He wasn't sophisticated or well-dressed, and he didn't shower me with gifts and compliments. I wanted a man who could cook (you already know how much I hated the kitchen), but Gabor, in the 12 years of his previous marriage and living in his big house, never even knew where the kitchen was. So, cooking for me? No... that wasn't going to happen.

He wasn't even spiritual!!!
But he was AWAKE!
He was CONSCIOUS!
That is why he was my perfect partner.

What Gabor really was couldn't possibly be on my list, as I didn't know someone like him even existed. When I was pursuing my mind-based spirituality, I manifested mind-based spiritual teachers. Until the moment of shutting off my mind with its interpretation and comparison activities, I couldn't possibly know what a real awakened person was. So, how could I have known to ask for someone like that. How could I have attracted that with a mind that is incapable of comprehending what is beyond its grasp?

It was the universe that knew exactly what I needed. Thus, in the mode of relinquishing my list with all its engraved and dreamed-up expectations, surrendering my thoughts and allowing things to unfold without any mental interference – the universe was finally able to deliver to me a partner that far exceeded any expectation that I could possibly have. For that I am eternally grateful.

A Conscious Relationship

> If one or both partners are committed to bypassing the
> mind – there am 'I' in their midst... as peace, harmony and
> unconditional love.

Gabor and I were recently interviewed by Anna Lena Eldoey
Nygaard, a spiritual coach and couple & family therapist from
Norway, about the topic of conscious relationships. Here are a
few excepts from this interview.

*Anna Lena: I am very interested in how awakening affects a
couple in a relationship. What is it like when both are conscious?
Also, when one of the partners is more ready than the other,
how does one deal with that in the best possible way?*

*Gabor: In the awakening process the most important thing
is to step out of the mind. You don't want to improve the mind.
You want to step out of it or what I call 'bypass' it. When you are
in a relationship you have your own mind and you also have
the other person's mind to deal with. Congratulations! It's ok...
there are some advantages.*

*Let's say you are able to bypass your mind slightly better than
your partner can, meaning - whatever the mind is saying, you
are able to bypass it and stay in your heart and go into your
inner Queendom, but your partner is not able to do the same.
Then it is your responsibility to lead the conversations and the
behaviors of the couple. It's your responsibility to go to that
peaceful space of your Queendom quickly and be there while
the mind of the other person is still moving.*

*So, you have already bypassed your own mind and now the
next step is to deal with your partner's mind. But you are not
really 'dealing' with that. You are 'bypassing' it as well. You are
simply BEING while the other (mind) stuff is going on. And in
time, the relationship usually gets fixed.*

Ten percent of the time the other person can't stand all this love and runs away. However, ninety percent of the time your partner's mind will calm down, and there is a special love that is being developed. So, someone has to take the responsibility of going to this silent 'place'. It could alternate – it doesn't always have to be your responsibility. It could be your partner's. Whoever gets to this place can stay there and from that perspective everything works.

If both partners' minds are running, if they are both unconscious and if they are competing – even if it is on a spiritual level – things just get worse and worse and worse. Someone, or both, have to get to that place where they can say, "Whatever is happening, my mind feels that I'm right, but I am conscious enough to say, 'ok, let's go to a different plateau, a different platform, from which we can attend this.'"

The way we do this is that 'I' go there. I don't force my partner to go to that plateau. I take the responsibility to calm down and to collapse into this loving being, even if my mind doesn't want to go to that place. Now something very powerful happens – in front of my partner, in front of my partner's mind, I am able to bypass my mind and go to God... to hold God's hand, so to speak. The personal power 'as' BEING increases a thousand-fold just because of that.

There is great benefit in being the leader in this process. It doesn't have to be you. It can alternate if two people are approximately on the same level. Sometimes I catch myself and I go there (inside) unconditionally, and at other times my partner does. This is a very powerful exercise for the leader as well as for the partner.

So, if you are in this kind of relationship, don't wait for your partner to cooperate. Just do it! Don't say, "Well, I am going to go into the 'now' when my partner goes into the 'now'." NO! "If she will be peaceful, I will be peaceful." NO! It's just you and God...NOW.

"I am going to God whether you like, whether society likes it, or not. I am holding God's hand even if it is not institutionally approved." The benefits of this are amazing and the effects on one's life are remarkable.

Anna Lena: How is it for you, Nurit, to live as a conscious couple?

Nurit: For me it is very valuable to be in a relationship with an awakened being like Gabor. It forces me to practice being present, being in my Queendom. It's like having a constant reminder to go within. Not that he has to keep telling me. He allows me to be as I am. But if I am not present when I am with him, I don't get him. He lives there, and I want to live where he lives. That's why we are married – so that we can live together. Living together is not restricted to an apartment. It is not restricted to a bed. It goes way beyond that.

Our relationship is not as personal as it is universal. When one is tuned into the inner being, the experience is more universal. It's not that I don't think of him as Gabor who is a person, a man who does this, that and the other. However, those things kind of take a back seat.

If I am not present and I am looking at him only as a person with a mind, I don't know him. I don't know who he is. We are so different. His background is miles away from mine. His taste in things is miles away from mine. But when I am present, it's not just that I know him – it's like I am looking at and being with myself. It actually feels like I am looking at myself.

My favorite practice is to speak with Gabor from presence. When I do that, it is a whole different story. When you are speaking with someone from presence, and they are speaking with you from presence the understanding is on such a deep level.

Gabor: Communicating from a non-conflict reality creates non-conflict, so there is very little friction if any. There might be a misunderstanding but very quickly it goes back to non-conflict. There is no drama.

Nurit: The other thing that I have found is that our relationship never gets old. Every moment is new. Every moment is fresh. In the past my relationships were not like that. We would get tired of each other and bored with each other. To others my current relationship may appear to be a boring one, but it is not. Boredom is in the mind. If we are present with each other and not in the mind, then we are not bored. There are no power struggles and there is no fighting. So, there is no make-up sex.

Gabor: *That's the biggest problem. (laughter)*

Nurit: We tried really hard to fight once, so that we can have make-up sex.

Gabor: *It didn't work!*

Nurit: Not at all. We didn't succeed. It was exhausting just to try to find something to argue about.

So, people who love excitement and drama in life might say that our relationship is boring, but I am never bored. Our conversations are very deep and never dull. It's not that we exchange a lot of information, but we have consistent realizations and discoveries as we go deeper inside while conversing. Every time we talk, there is a new understanding that comes up, which is actually how we created Gabor's book "Functional Silence: De-mystifying Awakening for the Spiritually Exhausted". [See Resource page to access this book.]

We would meet in a coffee shop and talk, and Gabor would have these downloads of information and ideas. When I would hear those ideas, I would be so amazed. And, of course, I could not hear those if I was not present. That was a great practice for me. This way the ideas became alive.

Anna Lena: *How was it when you met? You have been together for seven years now.*

Gabor: *[pointing to Nurit] You are more qualified to answer this question.*

Nurit: *[laughing and pointing at Gabor] Because he never had to change! It's true!*

We actually met ten years ago and have been together for seven. Initially when we met, we went out for about a month, and my mind was running and running and running. I had a tremendous spiritual ego at that time. I would lecture to him, but he never tried to impress me. I didn't understand this at first.

I got that there was something special about him because he has always listened from presence. In other words, there is no thought interruption when he listens, so it was like speaking into a pool of love or a pool of silence. This makes it is very easy to say anything that you need to say. You never feel like you are being judged.

So, it was fantastic from that perspective, and I was very aware that he knew the one thing that I was searching for. However, subconsciously, I didn't want my search to end. By that time, I was addicted to seeking, so I couldn't handle the relationship. I knew that if I kept on seeing him, I would have to change.

I found different excuses to put an end to the relationship. For example, I didn't like that he wore sandals with socks - big fashion faux pas! I didn't like that he lived in China-town and that he didn't have a car... the list goes on and on... So, those were my excuses, but after two and a half years I felt that I had to call him. That's when I realized that I had to stop my mind first in order to recognize Gabor. Shortly after that he was able to teach me and guide me into presence.

[The entire the story is in my book *The Blind Leading the Blonde on the Road to Freedom: Confessions of a Recovering Spiritual Junkie.* See Resource page to access it.]

Now my life is so different. Everything changed for the better. There is harmony and peace.

Gabor: Yes, there is a flow. There is a flow that is not there with people who are not conscious and whose minds are in constant negotiation mode and trying to make deals. We have none of that stress now. The mind is not involved unless we want it to be involved.

Say we want to talk about a subject, we bring up the information about the subject and we talk about that. When we have finished, we put it back on the shelf. There was a flow even while we were attending that subject. It is very peaceful and enjoyable.

All it takes is the simple awakening and activating the body as a transformational organ, and any relationship can be whatever you want it to be. Otherwise it can be hell.

> *If we need drama in our lives, we can just turn on the TV or go to the movies.*

What No Fire Can Destroy

Life happens. Whether we are awake or not, a conscious or an unconscious being – good and bad things still take place in our lives, as the pendulum of duality continues to swing. The only difference is in how we experience and 'be' with what is happening.

If we are asleep, we get all excited and energized when things are good, and we suffer when things go south. Upon awakening all this is altered. We feel joy that is peaceful when things are good without the temporary high and elation, and we may feel grief and sorrow when life throws us a tragic situation, but without the suffering that drags us to the next low.

So, although life does not suddenly become this wonderful thing with only good experiences and no challenges or hardships (as many spiritual people think), the underlying feeling changes. The duality of pleasure and suffering is replaced with the constant inner calm and stability of peace and satisfaction, from which easy and quick solutions arise, without the mind's narrative about the good or bad situation.

This is where true manifestation can take place and miracles happen. This is how life can in fact change for the better after awakening, and the changes are permanent. For this reason, one rarely feels the need to engage in deliberate creation. Between the ongoing inner satisfaction and being with the flow of the universe, there is hardly a need or a desire to ask for anything.

As I mentioned before, Gabor and I had a fire in our apartment, and just about everything was burned down. Fortunately, we were not home. Gabor was being interviewed downtown (Budapest), and the fire was going at the exact same time. It was put out by the time we got home. There were fire trucks, police cars and ambulances everywhere and the apartment was utterly black and reeking of soot and ashes.

All we had were the clothes on our backs and nowhere to sleep. This should have been an extremely disturbing experience for us. Through deepening into presence, the mind was not allowed to have its old ways. If it had, this would have turned into a major catastrophe, and there would have been tremendous emotional pain of loss, distress, worry, anxiety and everything that would accompany such a devastating occurrence.

Thus, our practice of turning within and bypassing the mind's commentary paid off big time. And even more so in my brief episode in the mall when we were in search for a mattress. Here was an opportunity to witness our gift in action and take it further by using this potentially painful situation to go deeper inside and rely on our inner being for resolution.

Sure enough, the events that followed were nothing short of a series of miracles and amazing manifestations. It turned out that Gabor's cousin, Eva Harsanyi, was headed to Germany for three days and invited us to stay at her apartment, which was just a few blocks away from our burned apartment.

This was great, but where would we go after three days? It could take weeks before we could find a new place to live. And here came the greatest miracle of all - we were able to find a new apartment within a day and a half. This is totally unheard of in a city like Budapest, where so many students come from all over the world and occupy many properties. The new apartment turned out to be less expensive, more suitable and in a much nicer area.

> *We never know why things happen... nor do we need to. All we can do is keep the real flame – the flame of silence and love in our hearts – ALIVE!*

Next, we received hundreds of emails, phone calls and messages filled with love and support and all kinds of offers. Friends and strangers showed up with bags and suitcases full of clothes, kitchen-ware, linens and more. Friends and relatives sent money that covered some other needs. We have never felt so loved and supported in our entire lives.

And best of all, in the midst of all the loss, the chaos, the painful situation, the confusion and devastation, the sense of peace and inner stillness was as strong as ever. This inspired us to make a short video called *What No Fire Can Destroy*. A couple of months after this video came out, we received an email from a student/friend who wrote that upon watching this video he had a complete healing of his sickness and pain. We never know why things happen... nor do we need to. All we can do is keep the real flame – the flame of silence and love in our hearts – ALIVE!

I Am Whole... What Else Can I Ask For?

Before I met Gabor, my daughter and I used to go for long walks with her dog during which, we would state our intentions and declare what we wished to manifest. We mostly followed the Abraham Hicks Law of Attraction method.

Several years ago, while Gabor and I were still living in Toronto, we went to visit my daughter at her home. Upon arriving, she asked me if I would do the same kind of manifestation or co-creating session with her as we used to do, since she wanted to manifest more money.

"I would be happy to." I replied. "Why don't we do it a bit differently this time. Let's do it the way Gabor taught me."

"Sure." she agreed.

So, Gabor and I sat at my daughter's large kitchen table, and both she and her husband joined us. Gabor began to guide us and directed us on going inside the body. Not sure how much time passed, since we were all so deep inside and time no longer existed for us. At one-point Gabor asked each of us to state what we wished to manifest while remaining in our peaceful inner presence. When it came to my daughter's turn, she was speechless.

"What is it that you want to manifest?" Gabor asked her after a long silent pause.

"Nothing!" she said when she could finally speak. "I feel completely whole at this moment. I don't feel any need."

The universe is not a mind reader, but it sure seems to know what we feel when our minds are still.

It has the intelligence and dexterity to give us more than our minds can possibly conceive.

Chapter Eight

Back to Utopia

Just Imagine...

> "*You may say I'm a dreamer*
> *But I'm not the only one*" **John Lennon**

John Lennon was right – he was not the only one. I too dream from time to time, but not so much about what I want or need for my life to be better. Knowing that the inner satisfaction trumps all else, and that I can go into my Queendom anytime, I rarely feel the need for improvements in my own life.

Nonetheless, I would love to see changes on a global scale. I am not talking about becoming an activist or even wishing for a certain party to win an election. I know full well, that the only way to bring about change on any scale is through presence and inner dwelling.

I often lay awake at night wondering what it would be like to wake up the next morning and find that every human being is awake... truly awake... not just suddenly becoming a good person with lofty intentions, but living in and from the place of peace and silence.

Gabor and I have great conversations during our morning coffee time or at our favorite coffee shop. I often record these exchanges, since they provide great inspiration and insights. One of those mornings we spoke about what we imagined the world would be like if we were to live in a conscious society where everyone was fully awake to their true nature.

I share this conversation with you here not as a means to offer our opinions, but rather as a platform to set an intention for the world we live in. My objective here is to include you in our "wouldn't it be nice if..." session, with the hopes that you will be inspired to participate in our quest for a more enlightened world.

Me: *So, what would be the new way of being?*

Gabor: It is actually shameful that we have to call it a 'new' way of being. There is nothing new about it. As a matter of fact, it is so old. It is as old as the Golden Age, where humanity didn't have any programming. It only had coding by God or the universal intelligence. Humanity then was still innocent, and we saw the world as it is instead of through programmed colored glasses.

When our computer is full of spyware or viruses it suddenly starts choking and is no longer able to function. Luckily, in most computers there is a re-set program that re-sets it to the original state. This is what a genuine teacher does – re-sets a person to their original being.

Me: I wonder what it would be like if everyone was re-set. What if we all could live that way... being re-set to our original being?

Gabor: For each being life would feel good. It would feel great to be alive. There would be no such thing as a problem and there would be no enemies. Every human's basic operation mode would be the unconditional love upon which everything else is placed.

Humanity's common difficulties as they exist today would be non-existent. There would be no conflicts. Things like wars, spies, police, law enforcement agencies, lawyers, prisons, etc. would be irrelevant and therefore extinct. We would not need an ID card or a passport to prove who we are.

Me: I guess there would be no need for security at airports and embassies... no borders, no legal systems, no crime, no rape... what would they talk about on CNN? They would have to shut down or just give the weather and sports reports all day. Even good news would be obsolete, since there would be no good or bad in a world that is not duality-based.

Gabor: The new human would operate through a peaceful intelligence that is common to everyone. There would be no sense of lack of anything or any kind of greed, jealousy or competitiveness. There would be no need for manipulation.

Me: I suppose the banking system would change... even collapse.

Gabor: The whole banking system as it exists today is set up in such a way that it promotes fear, slavery and evil through high interest rates, impossible mortgages and collection agencies. To the banks we are nothing but a ledger entry. These systems will no longer be able to chain us in the new utopian world.

There is an infinite amount of inventions that have already been developed. These have the ability to infinitely help humanity in agriculture, in health, in energy and in many other ways. Currently they are hidden and withheld from us. When these inventions were made they were bought out by big corporations and, because those corporations have already invested millions and millions of dollars in the old systems, these new inventions were kept under lock and key.

When the walls of duality, conflict, greed and fear come tumbling down, those inventions will become available to us. They will be coming out of hiding and will provide humanity with unlimited resources. Humanity will benefit greatly and may no longer need to use systems like banks, collection agency and insurance companies.

Me: People will no longer need to be enslaved by nine-to-five jobs, where they mostly work from seven-to-seven in order to beat the competition and ensure that they don't lose the chains of their false security.

What do you suppose the governments would be like?

Gabor: At this moment we can't really know what a new moment will be like. We can only speculate for the purpose of setting an intention for what we see as an ideal situation. So, we don't know how it will be or how the systems for running a country will manifest in a new world, in which all are awake and living in the peaceful platform of love.

However, what we can be absolutely sure of without a shadow of doubt is that decisions will be made from a whole different perspective, an entirely transformed level, and they will be made at the moment that they need to be made. At that time, I suppose the role of the new type of government would be to coordinate and communicate.

Right now, the governments are in a law enforcement mode. They feed on greed, fear, competition, ambition, manipulation, control, and so forth. It's not like there are evil governments out there, and we are here as a population that is good.

Humanity at this point is not capable of electing politicians and leaders who could lead us out of the madness that we find ourselves in. In its current state, humanity is only capable of fear and greed. Our lives are built out of fear. So, when we go to vote, for example, we are only capable of and willing to reflect our own fears. The government is a 100% reflection of humanity at this point and it is not a separate evil entity.

Me: *This is precisely why it is imperative for more and more people to awaken to their original being. There must be individual change before we can expect an entity like a government to change.*

THE FEMININE PRINCIPLE: THE KEY TO AWAKENING FOR MEN AND WOMAN

YOU ARE NOT GOING TO BELIEVE THIS!!!

As I am typing this conversation in this book, the financial news just came on the TV. I couldn't believe my ears.

They were talking about the recent meeting between the North Korean and the South Korean leaders (April 2018) who decided to go towards peace and de-nuclearization.

The headlines read:
"NO PROFIT IN PEACE!"

Then they proceeded to list the loses of value to the following giant weapon manufacturers:
Lockheed Martin 2.5%
Northrop Grumman 3.4%
General Dynamics 3.8%
Raytheon 3.6%
Boeing 1%
The collective loss of value due to the 'threat' of peace amounted to – $10.2 billion!

Holy shit! Did I just hear that killing makes for good money?
What kind of world are we living in?
There is something inherently evil about this.
What war will they drum up next?

Me: *Of course, once society if freed from the mind and its insanity, the need for psychiatrists and therapist would also be outdated. When humans finally value that special feeling that springs from inside, who will be there to ask, "How does that make you feel?"*

Gabor: *Parents will be totally present with their children right from the start. They would not have the need to feel superior to their children based on more life experience. Parent and child will hold equal value as present beings and will learn from each* *other. As they both live in the moment, there will be no need to force useless information down the child's throat. Kids will learn what they feel attracted to learn.*

Me: *And since children will no longer be raised and educated to be slaves at a nine-to-five job, school hours might change. Education may never be 'timed' again. What if it was just a moment-to-moment learning and discovery?*

Gabor: *Most likely it will.*

Me: *And the battle of the sexes will also be extinct.*

Gabor: *Men and women alike will have the perfect balance of male and female energies. They will bear the masculine qualities that will enable them to analyze, make decisions, take charge, organize, lead, etc. as well as the feminine qualities of compassion, allowing, nurturing, intuiting, surrendering, etc. They will co-exist in harmony, unconditional love, cooperation and peace.*

I hope you will join us in our liberating mission of individual and global awakening and inner peace. We feel that this is the course that the universe is now taking. Acquiring more and more money, positions, knowledge, accolades, and even spirituality have already lost a great deal of their value in the large scheme of things. There is a huge universal movement in the direction of simplicity and moment-to-moment living, as our original being pushes forward to be recognized and integrated.

Gabor and I are here to help in any way we can with this transition and inevitable transformation that is sweeping humanity in ever-growing speed. We are just a website or an email away. We would love to hear from you and have you join our loving family.

About the Author

Nurit Oren, CPCC, is a Canadian Certified Professional Co-Active Coach, a Certified Witz Management / Leadership Trainer and a Certified Art of Transformation Guide.

Over the past 20 years, Nurit has helped countless individuals from all walks of life make life-changing decisions from the heart, by creating a safe space for inner wisdom and courage to guide them in the direction that is right for them, and free them from being stuck in unwanted situations.

Nurit is also a public speaker, an award-winning playwright and the author of *"The Blind Leading the Blonde on the Road to Freedom: Confessions of a Recovering Spiritual Junkie"*. This book is the story of her 40 years of intense spiritual seeking in several countries and with many teachers; the mistakes, the pitfalls and the elusive bliss along the way. It also describes how she finally found the truth after meeting Gabor who guided her into the "No-Thought Presence", upon which the realization dawned on her that all her previous pursuits were none other than a mind with an ego attempting to become enlightened.

Nurit is also the co-author of Gabor Harsanyi's book *"Functional Silence: De-mystifying Awakening for the Spiritually Exhausted"*. She manages Gabor's activities and programs and also interviews awakened beings and spiritual leaders from all over the world.

For more information on Nurit please visit:
www.gaborharsanyi.com

To access the books mentioned above, see the Resource page in the front of this book.

About Gabor Harsanyi

Gabor Harsanyi is an awakening coach who frees people from thought addiction, allowing consciousness to awaken and to become the real guide. He is the author of *Functional Silence: De-mystifying Awakening for the spiritually exhausted.*

Gabor nearly lost his life escaping from communist Hungary at the age of 18. He arrived in Canada with a single minded and insatiable thirst for his first love – power and material wealth. At the age of 30 he was already a multi-millionaire, had his black belt in Hap-Kido, and had degrees in business and engineering. However, he was not at all happy.

And so, Gabor turned to his 2nd love – spirituality. He resided with and was initiated by a Shaman in Ecuador and lived in a forest in the U.S., attending Ramtha's School of Enlightenment. He also studied with teachers such as Burt Harding and Bob Proctor and took every new age seminar within shooting distance. All these served as soul searching pacifiers with an occasional glimmer of "What a great experience! If only I could hang on to it a bit longer."

Finally, at the age of 40, Gabor found his true Master – suffering. His suffering came in the forms of heartbreak, the loss of his family and his entire fortune, and suicidal depression. Through the grace of this newfound master, Gabor was now able to surrender to his 3rd and ultimate love – Presence, the silence of nothing, where the capitulated mind takes a back seat and becomes the servant.

Having deepened his presence and integrating it into his life, Gabor developed many techniques and the ability to teach the indescribable. For the past 10 years, he has been offering seminars and private sessions, online and in several countries around the globe. In these sessions, Gabor not only guides people and teaches the techniques he has developed, but he also helps them deal with the mind's onslaughts by proxy. In Hungary he is known as the Master of Silence.

For more information on Gabor please visit:
www.gaborharsanyi.com

To access Gabor's book, see the Resource page in the front of this book.

www.ingramcontent.com/pod-product-compliance
Lightning Source LLC
Chambersburg PA
CBHW071749120626
46550CB00002B/720